To my darlin Gill. on her 44th

Whitby 2006.

Oh such a perfect ♪ day ♪

Im glad I spent it with you.....

... and you know the rest.

All my love

Mel ☺

381. TMD. Always.

SCENE THROUGH A LENS

Photographs by Michael J. Shaw

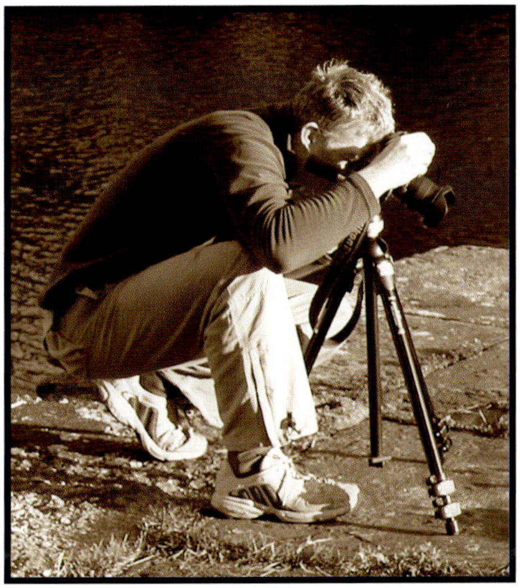

Thanks to my beautiful wife, Tricia

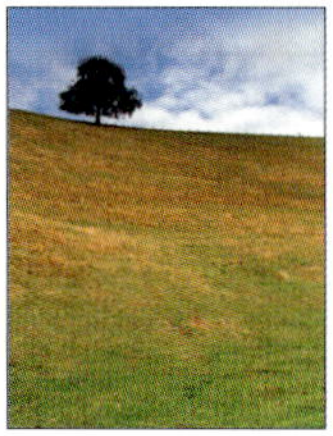

Cover photograph 'The Tree'
Taken near Lockton, North Yorkshire.
October 2002 Canon D60

ISBN Number: 0 9541860 2 8

Introduction

This book has been born from a passion for digital photography; not just 'conventional' photography, but the exciting new medium that has given so many people like me, a fresh and revitalised interest in image taking.

Photography was a serious hobby as a teenager, but after that, I only ever used a camera for holiday snaps.

Until the year 2000...when my wife, Tricia bought me a digital camera for Christmas and from that day forward I became 'hooked'.

My father, Bill Shaw was a professional photographer for 25 years, so I grew up in a world of cameras, smelly chemicals in the darkroom and watching him take his stunning black and white portraits.

Another major influence on my picture taking must be Frank Meadow Sutcliffe; I have lived and worked with his superb Victorian photographs all my life. I am now the curator of the Sutcliffe collection at Whitby museum.

Joe Cornish is also on my list of heroes! I refer above to 'conventional' photography as apposed to digital, but I think it will be a long time before pixels can compete with Joe's large format film and the exquisite quality of his landscapes.

An exhibition, titled 'Scene through a lens' was launched at the same time as the publication of this book. It will be touring galleries throughout the country. For further details please contact *Norlandscapes*.

I hope this book will inspire and encourage photographers to invest in a digital camera.
It is not just the taking of the photograph, but what you can achieve afterwards. On that subject I would like to say that very few of the images in this book have been manipulated to any great extent, apart from adjusting exposure etc.

Michael J. Shaw

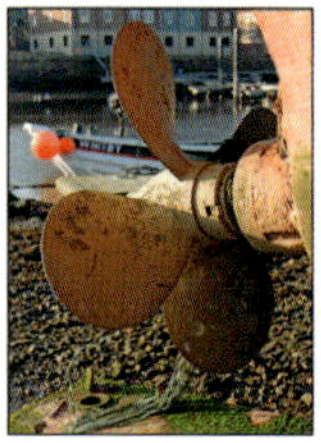

2

Propeller

Taken early morning on Whitby marina. A wide angle, close-up view of a propeller.

May 2004 Nikon D100

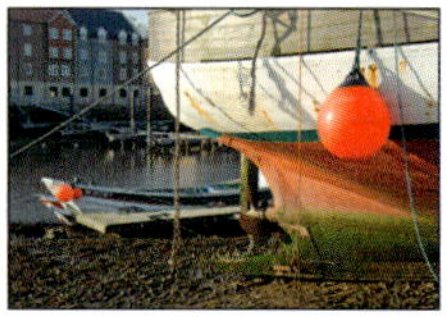

3

Red Buoy

Whitby marina with the newly constructed Whitehall Landing in the background.

May 2004 Nikon D100

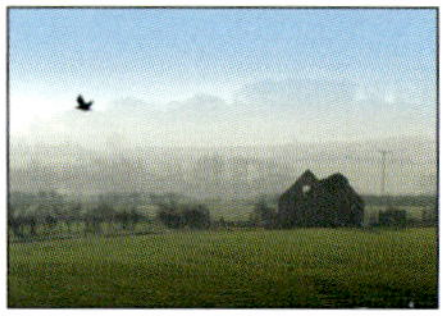

4

As the crow flies

Derelict barn in the afternoon mist on a farm near Ruswarp, Whitby.

Feb. 2003 Nikon D100

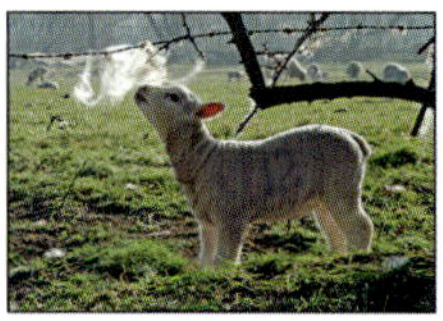

5

Pure New Wool

Early dawn sunshine, highlighting the back of a new spring lamb.

March 2003 Nikon D100

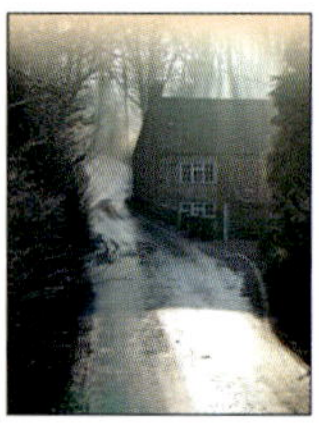

6

Early morning frost, Glen Esk

Taken towards 'Danger bank', a steep hill on a tight corner.
One of the earliest photographs of this collection.

Jan. 2001 Nikon Coolpix 880

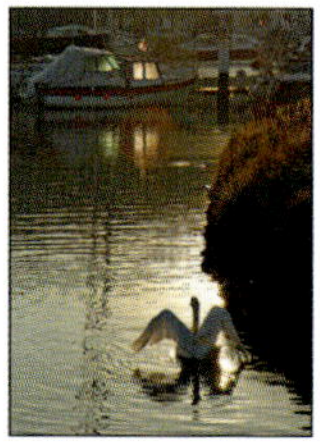

7

Spread your wings

A white swan in Whitby harbour, with Church street across the river. Taken towards the early morning light.

Oct. 2003 Nikon D100

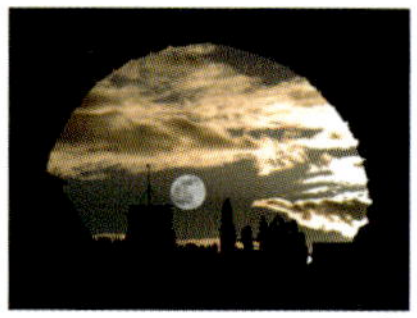

8

Through the keyhole

From 'spion kop' looking at St. Mary's church and Whitby Abbey, silhouetted against a dramatic sky.

Oct. 2003 Nikon D100

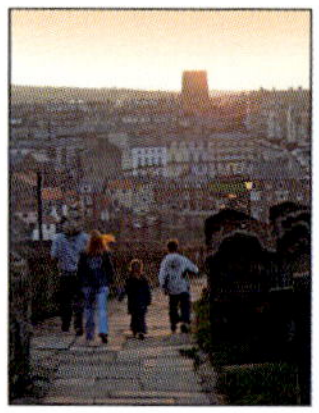

9

Top of the 199 steps

St. Mary's churchyard above the 199 steps. Warm evening sunlight, over the roof tops of Whitby with St. Hilda's church standing proud on the skyline.

March 2004 Nikon D100

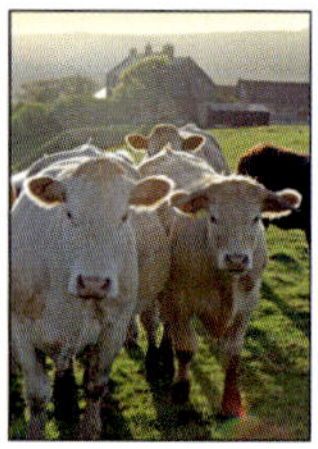

10

Herd the news?

Taken between Hinderwell and Staithes. Boulby potash mine in the background, the deepest mine in Europe.
The low evening sun creates dramatic backlighting.

April 2002 Canon D60

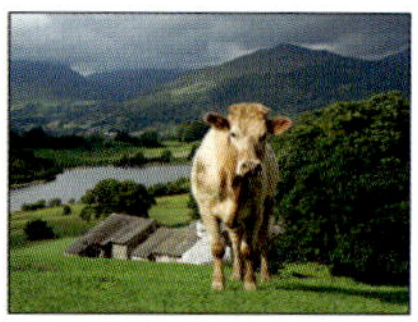

11

Curious cow

From Beatrix Potter's farm near Hawkshead, with Windermere in the distance.

June 2003 Nikon D100

Old Goat
A wide angle view of
this dear old goat,
taken near Roxby.

July 2003 Canon IXUS

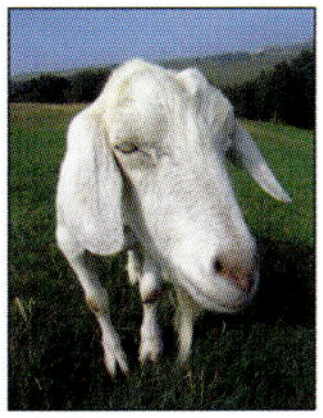
12

Fowl play
Turkeys, chickens and peacocks
all happily strutting in the
afternoon sunshine.
Sept. 2003 Nikon D100

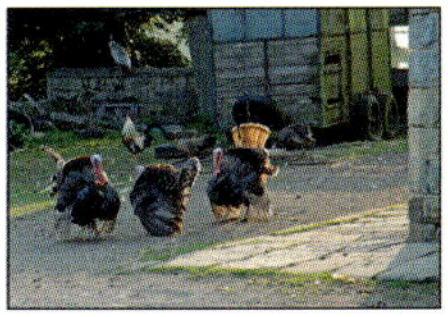
13

Venetian arcade
Early morning, before the crowds
in the shade of the arcade, off the
Piazza San Marco, Venice.

B & W with spot colour on the red vest.
Sept. 2003 Nikon D100

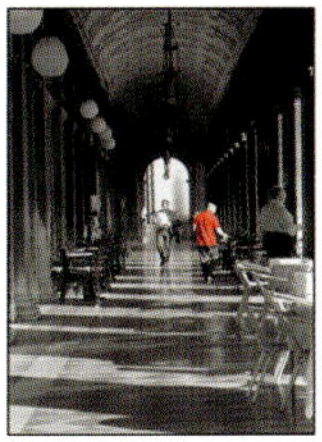
14

Under the marble bridge
Ferro of gondola appearing from under the
bridge... but who is on board?
The prongs of the ferro represent
the six different areas of Venice.

Sept. 2003 Nikon D100

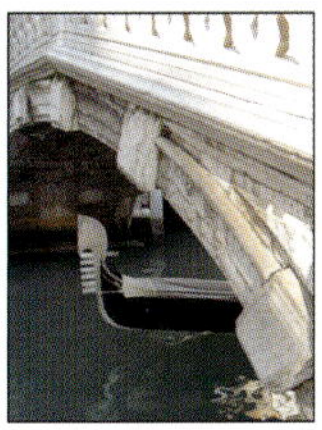
15

Grand Canal, Venice
Sunrise from the Accademia bridge
towards the Salute. The Grand Canal
divides the city into two equal halves.
Sept. 2003 Nikon D100

16

The Gondolier
Wearing the traditional Venetian
attire, this gondolier is transporting
tourists across the Grand Canal.
Gondolas are all 10.87m long
and 1.42m wide at the broadest point.
Sept. 2003 Nikon D100

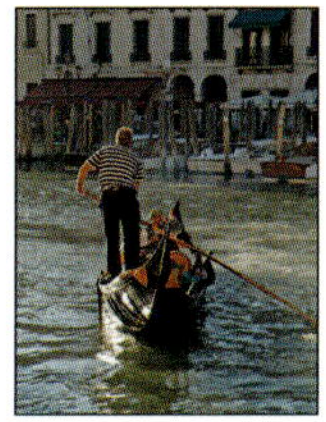
17

Brass band, Egton show
Two members of the award winning
Lockwood Brass band at Egton
horse and agricultural show in 2003.
The band is based at Lingdale, Cleveland.

August 2003 Nikon D100

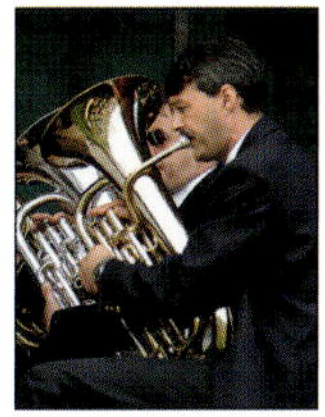
18

Top dog
Sheepdogs still vying for attention
even after a hard day working
on a farm in the Lake District.

June 2003 Nikon D100

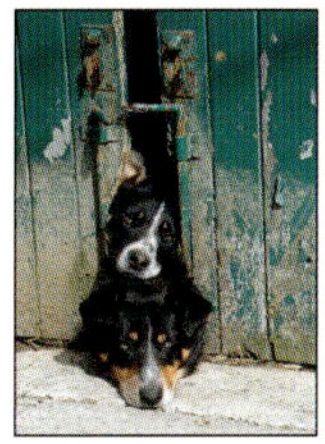
19

A new dawn
A tranquil river scene at dawn on the
morning of the eclipse of the sun.
From Ruswarp bridge.
May 2003 Nikon D100

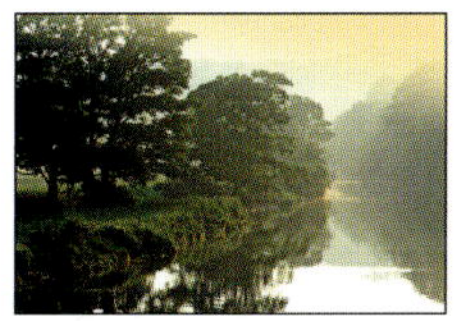
20

On reflection...
Mirror image on a flat calm river.
Pleasure boats on the Esk at Ruswarp.
The river banks are a haven for assorted
wildlife - herons, cormorants, swans
and otters to name but a few.
Sept. 2003 Nikon D100

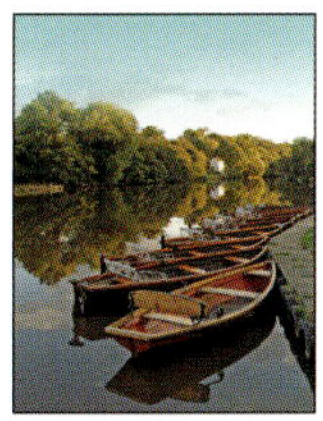
21

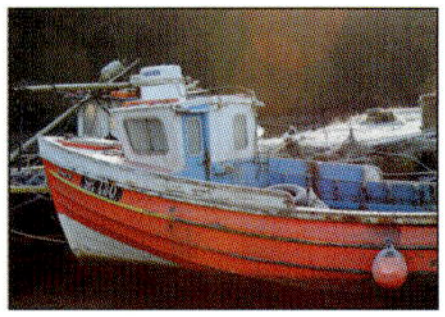

22

Red lipstick on the old girl
A grounded boat in the freezing cold of a December morning. Taken near the old gas works at Whitby.
Dec. 2003 Nikon D100

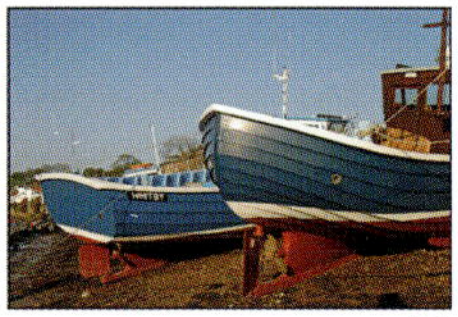

23

Blue boats, Whitby marina
Fishing cobles standing ashore, set against a blue sky.
An early morning shot.

May 2004 Nikon D100

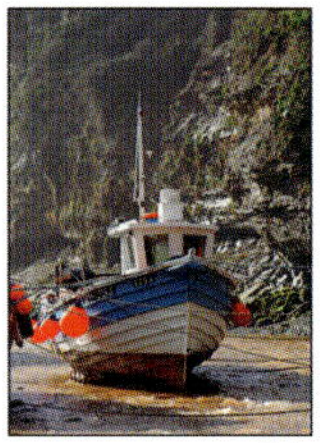

24

Staithes beck

Taken at noon, a fishing boat in brown water after heavy rain. The mighty Cowbar cliff of Staithes provides the backdrop.

Feb. 2004 Nikon D100

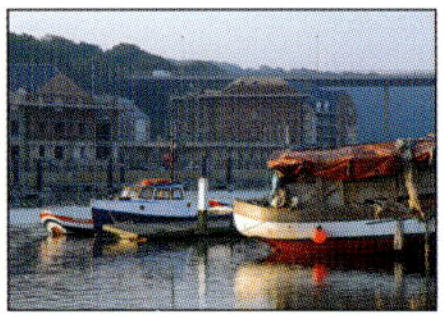

25

Whitehall landing
Whitby's harbourside development, under construction below the high level bridge. Colourful reflections ripple in the foreground.
Oct. 2003 Nikon D100

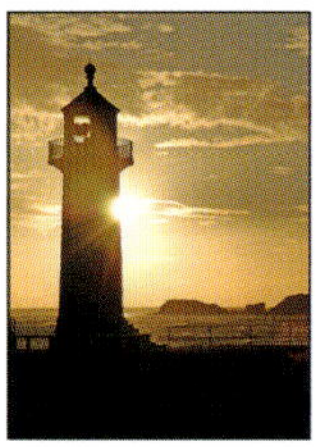

26

Sunrise
Whitby's East pier lighthouse was added in 1854 to the ancient East pier. The East and West piers provide safe passage into the harbour from the North sea.

Oct. 2003 Nikon D100

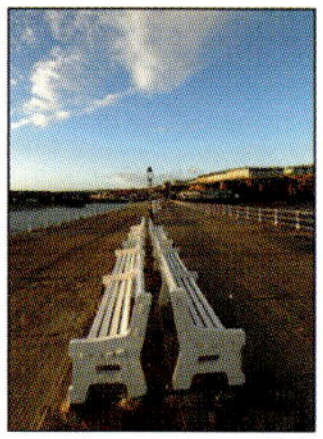

27

West pier, Whitby
A very wide angle lens has been used to create an unusual perspective of the benches.
The Royal Hotel can be seen bathed in early morning sunlight.

Oct. 2003 Nikon D100

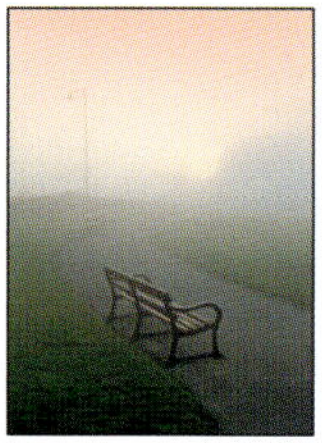

28

Misty sunset

Royal crescent, Whitby in the mist.
The setting sun burning through the coastal fog.

March 2003 Canon IXUS

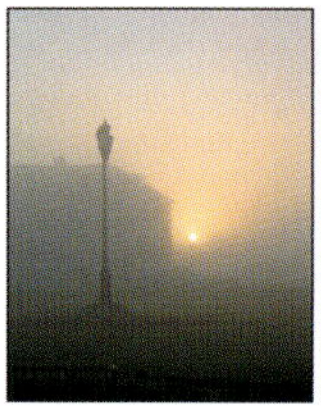

29

Crescent gardens, Whitby
A simple composition of a lamp post in mist.
The evening sunset creates unusual lighting conditions.

March 2003 Canon IXUS

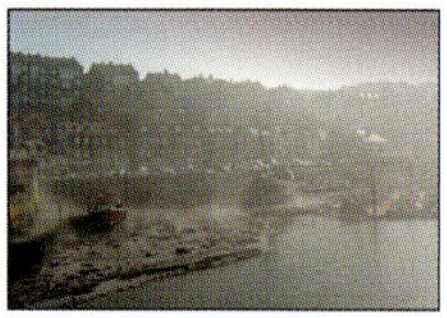

30

Misty sands
View from the swing bridge, Whitby.
Misty sands on the left shore near an area known locally as 'Tin Ghaut'.
March 2003 Canon IXUS

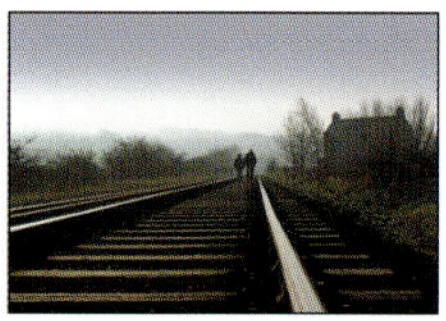

31

On the right track
A low wide angle perspective of the railway track.
Whitby to Middlesbrough line.

Feb. 2003 Canon IXUS

Two bridges
Sunrise near Spital Bridge, Whitby.
The quality of light very early in the morning gives this photograph a mellow tone. There are also strong shadows and luminous highlights.
Oct. 2003 Nikon D100

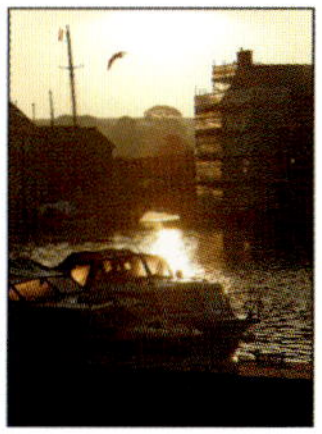

32

Warm dawn
This is one of the photographers' favourite images in this book.
Taken from Whitby marina in early morning sunlight.

Oct. 2003 Nikon D100

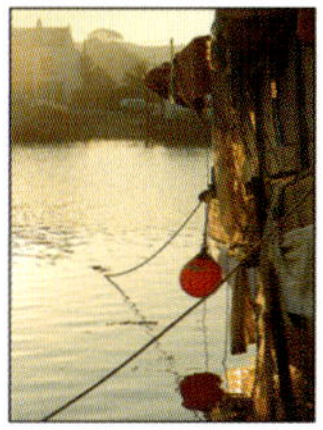

33

Partial eclipse, Whitby
At 4.50 a.m. on the 31st May 2003, showing the East pier extension.
Never before in recorded history has the Yorkshire coast witnessed a partial eclipse of the sun.
May 2003 Nikon D100

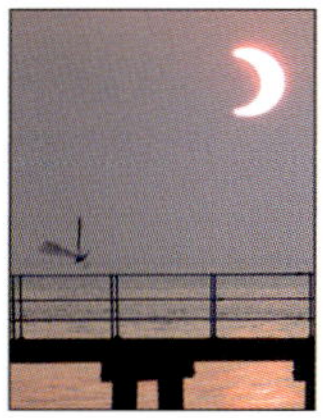

34

Green Lane, Whitby
This is an ideal example of being in the right place at the right time and having a camera with you!

Frosty winter afternoon.

Feb. 2001 Nikon Coolpix 880

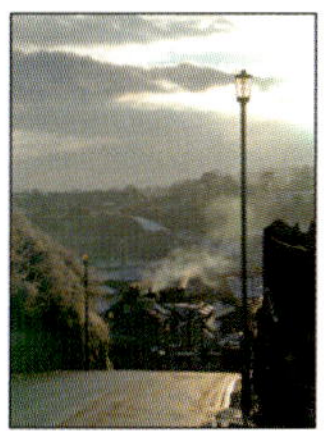

35

Power wash
Whitby marina provides a wealth of opportunities for the artist and photographer with the ever changing activities and lighting conditions.

Oct. 2003 Nikon D100

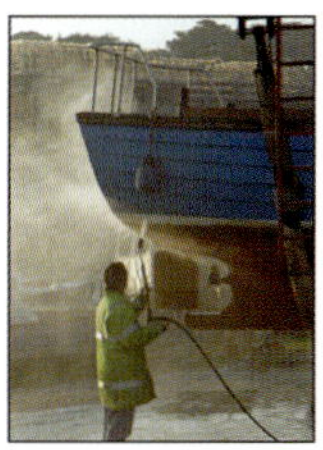

36

Cold front
Early morning, heavy frost at the 'Bog Hall' area of Whitby.
The prow of the boat encrusted with hoar frost crystals.

Dec. 2003 Nikon D100

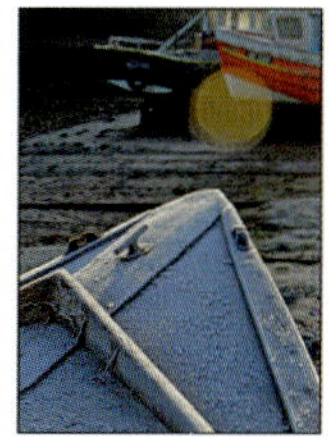

37

Grasmere
A restful scene in the Lake District.
Taken in dull conditions between showers that give the verdant growth to this area.

Aug. 2002 Canon D60

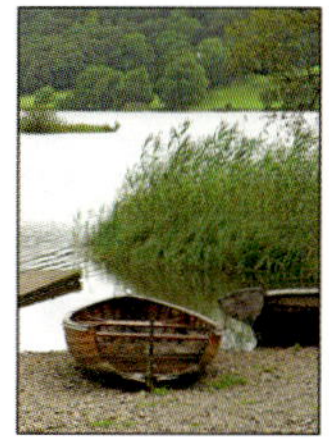

38

Under the willow tree
Boats on the river, Bergerac, France.
The graceful willow above the water creates a flowing arch for the vessels.
Dappled sunlight in foreground.

June 2002 Canon D60

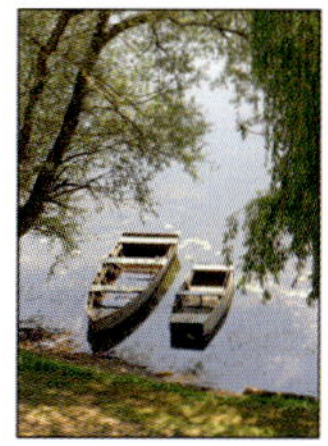

39

Winter bonfire
The sun and smoke combine to envelope the gentleman tending his allotment. Behind him is the Plantagenet Castle of Helmsley, now in the custody of English Heritage.

Feb. 2004 Nikon D100

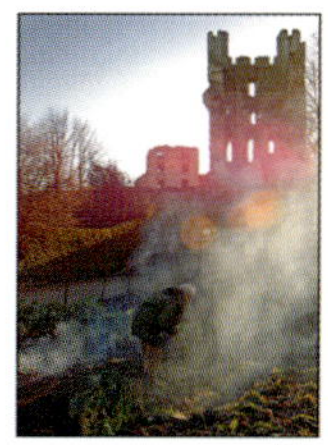

40

Running deer
An action shot showing the advantage of an SLR digital.
The quick response of this type of camera is a boon in these situations.
Aug. 2003 Nikon D100

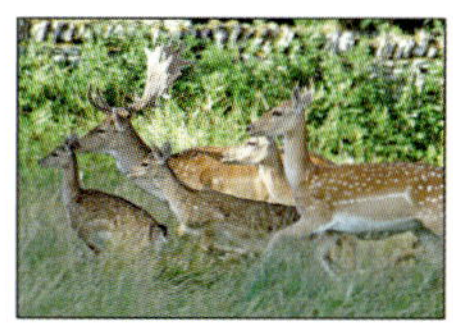

41

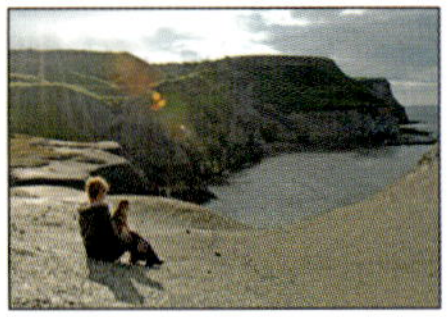
42

Sea of tranquility
'The moon walk', so called as this area resembles the surface of the moon. Nothing grows on these slopes, part of a cliff-top walk above Sandsend, Whitby.
Sept. 2003 Nikon D100

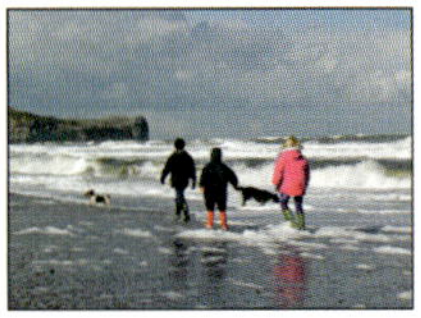
43

Bright new day
A bracing walk along the beach at Sandsend. The dark clouds emphasize the bright reflections along the white surf.
March 2001 Nikon Coolpix 880

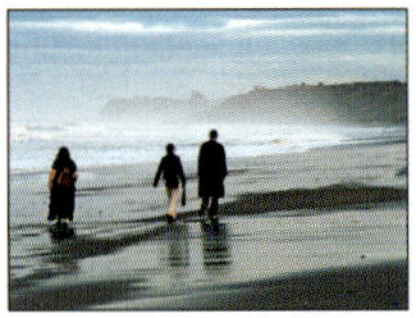
44

Sea spray
Walking away from Sandsend towards Whitby on a wet azure beach. Beyond the sea spray is the Gothic Whitby Abbey.
Sept. 2003 Nikon D100

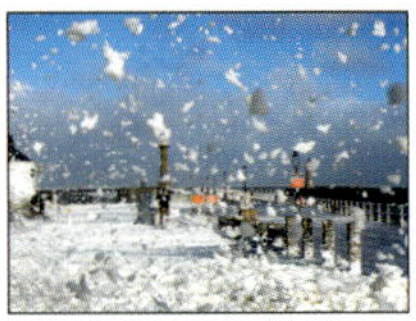
45

Foaming at the harbour mouth
The froth was attributed to a combination of plankton and very rough seas. Taken outside Whitby R.N.L.I. museum.
Jan. 2003 Nikon D100

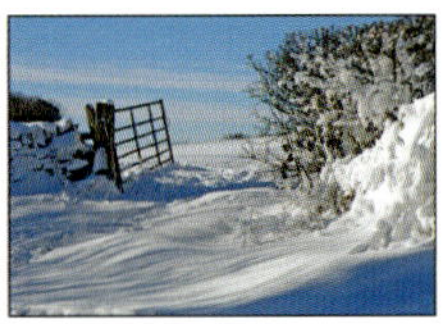
46

Winter gateway
Between Egton and Glaisdale. A rare, crisp, dry winters day. After heavy snowfall, strong shadows create sinewy effects.
Jan. 2004 Nikon D100

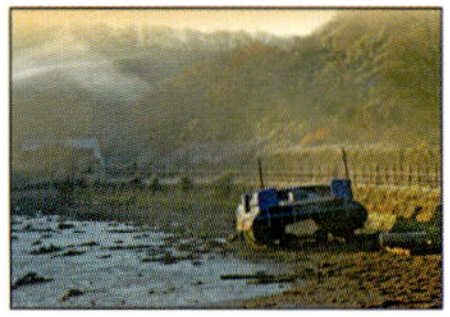
47

Frosty morning, Whitby
This photograph shows how frost, sun and smoke combine to give special atmosphere. On the river Esk.
Dec. 2003 Nikon D100

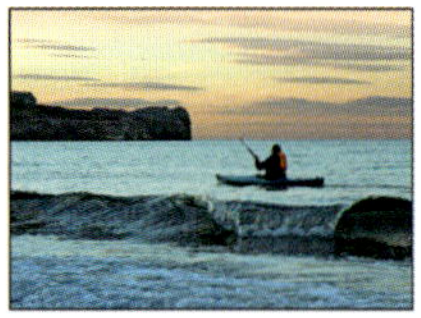
48

On the crest of a wave
A man in a canoe at Sandsend, on a calm sea with a beautiful sky at sunset.

Aug. 2003 Nikon D100

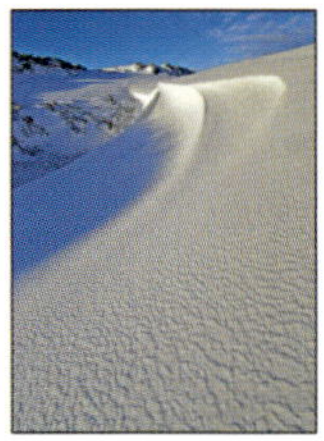
49

Big snow
Heavy snow on Whinstone Ridge, near Goathland (Heartbeat country). Waist deep in snow to achieve; this photograph really captures the great outdoors.

Jan 2004 Nikon D100

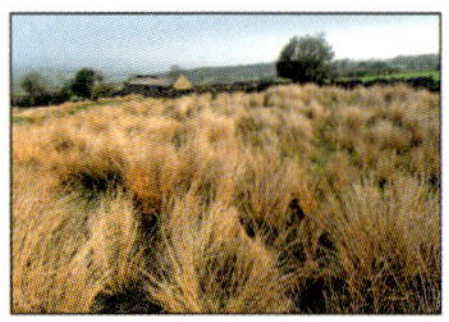
50

Green End, Goathland
Very wide angle landscape view of wild grasses on the dramatic North Yorkshire Moors.

April 2004 Nikon D100

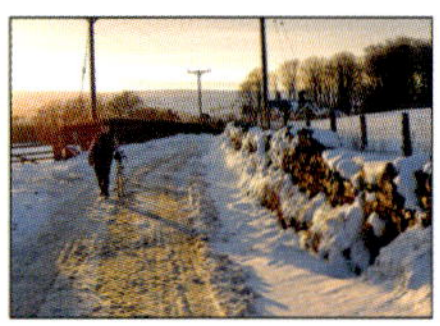
51

End of the day
The setting sun near Egton. Just passable after heavy snow, the track is bathed in a golden sunset glow.
Jan. 2004 Nikon D100

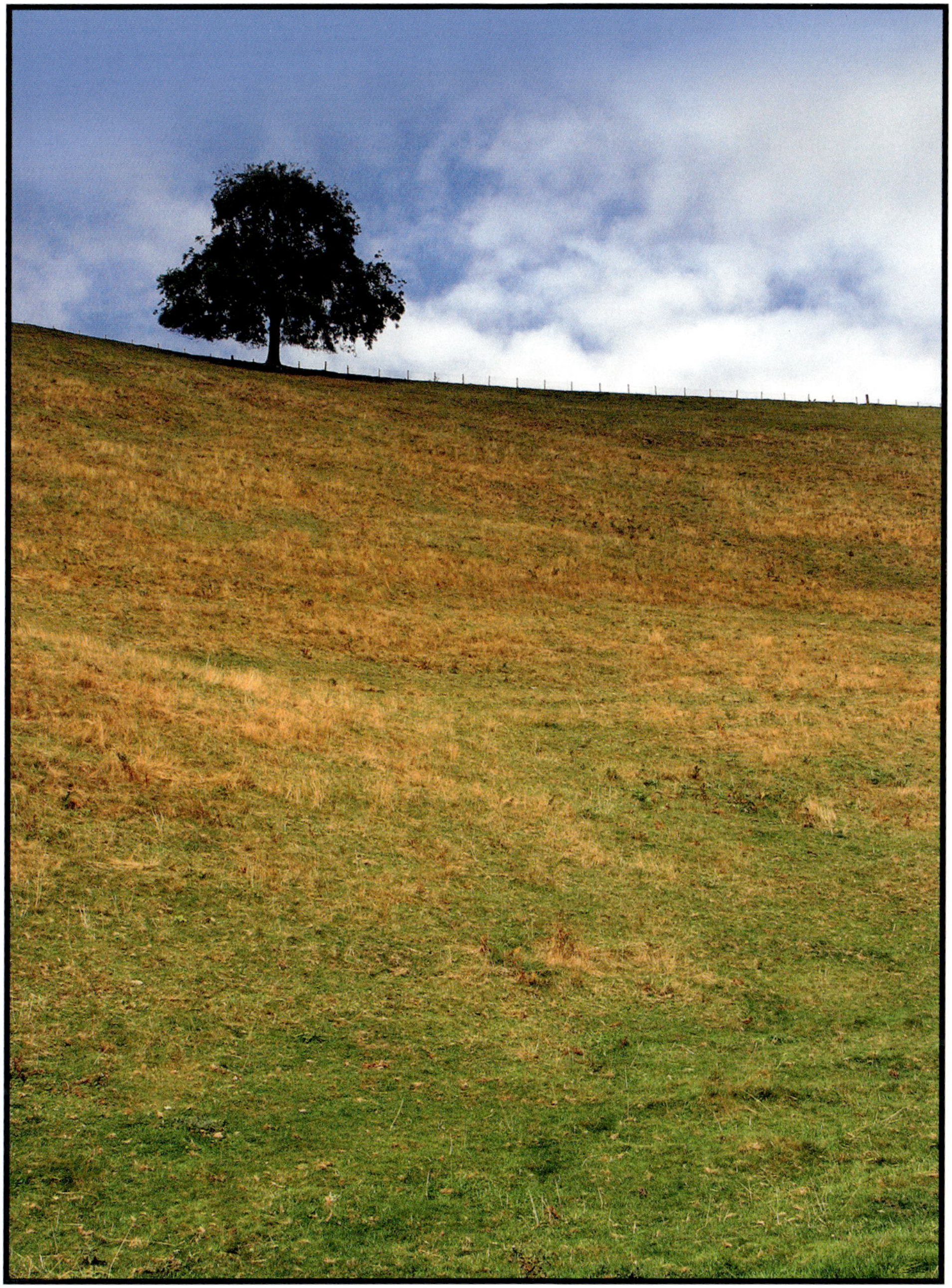

'The Tree'

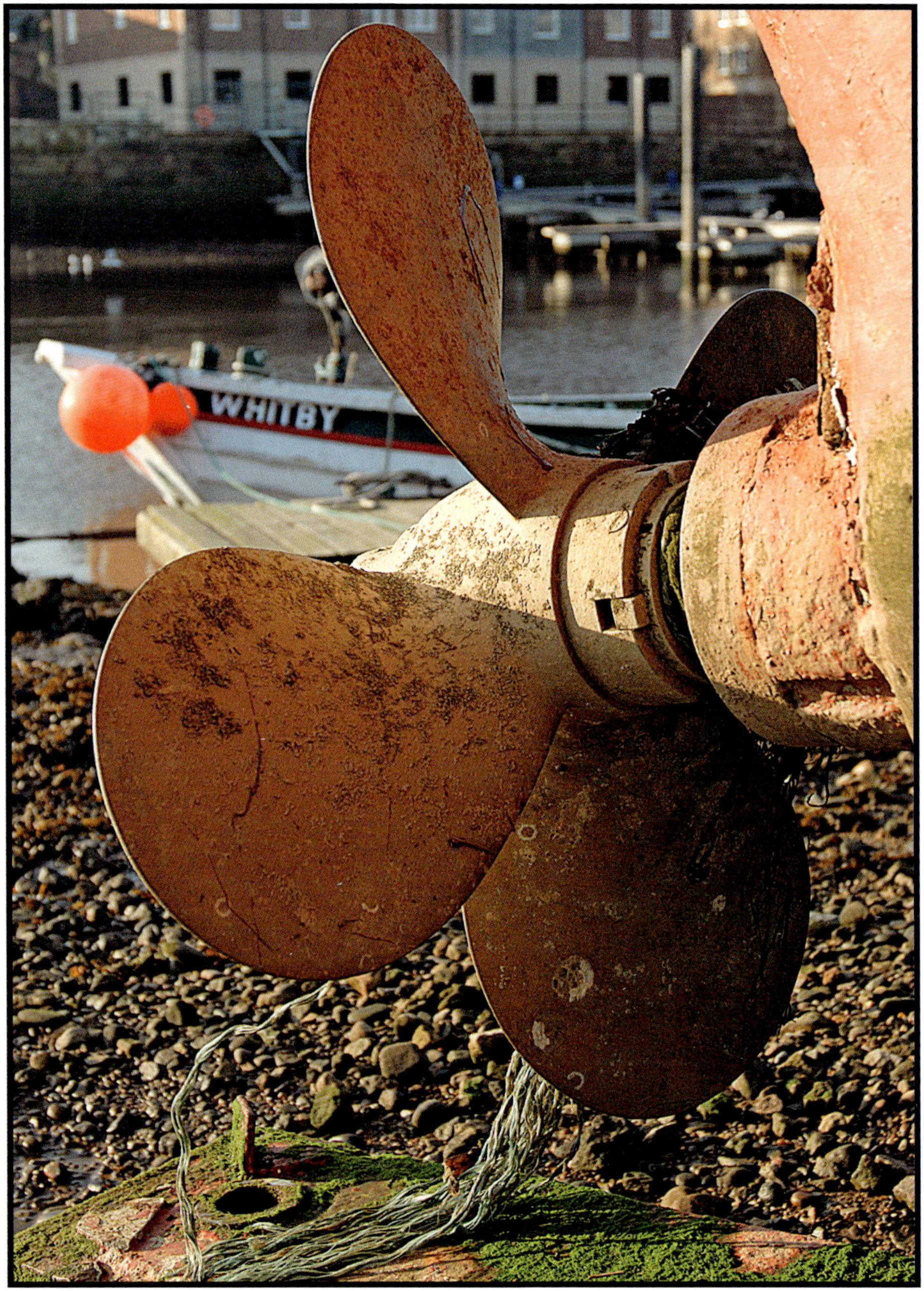

'Propeller'

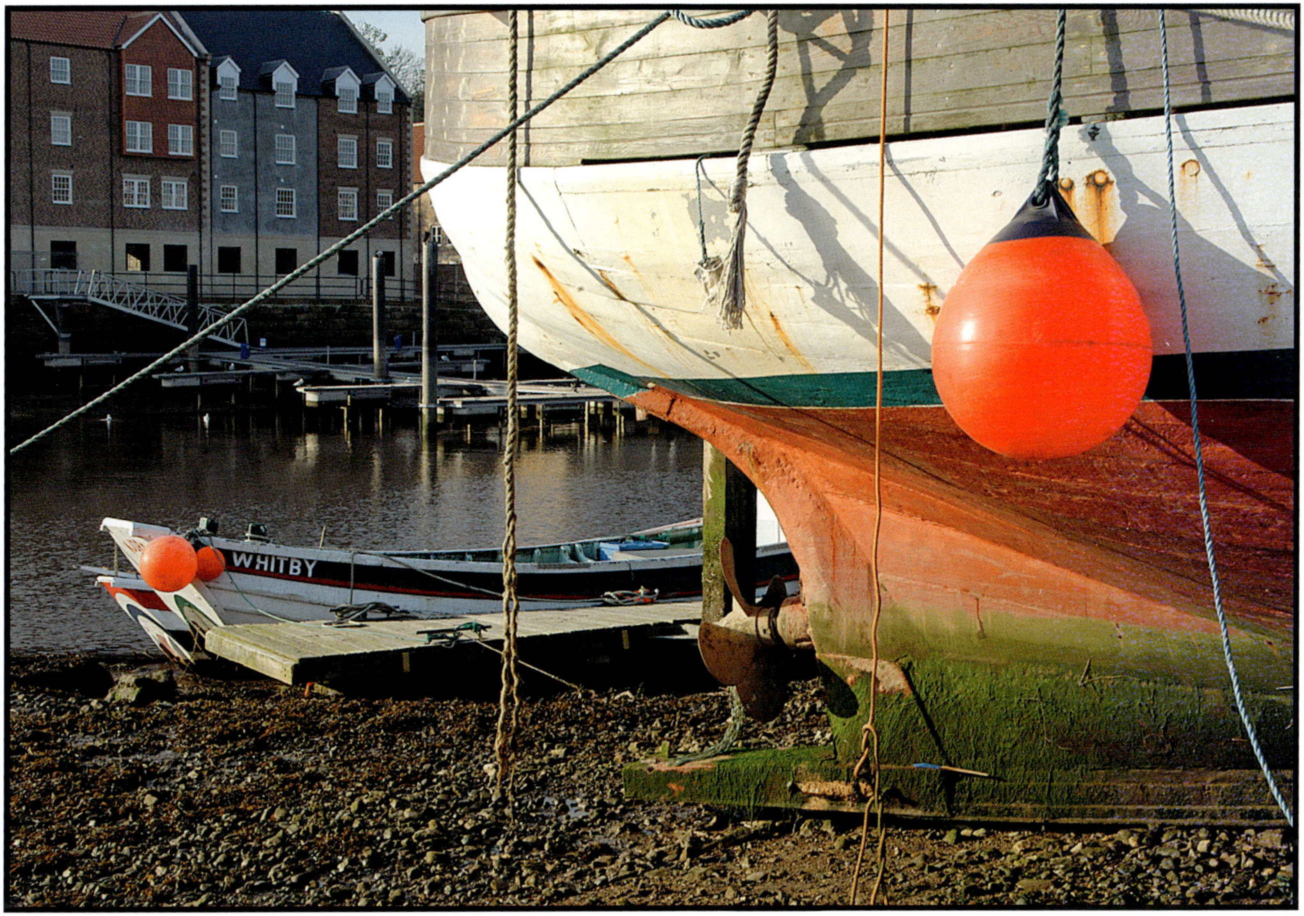

'Red Buoy'

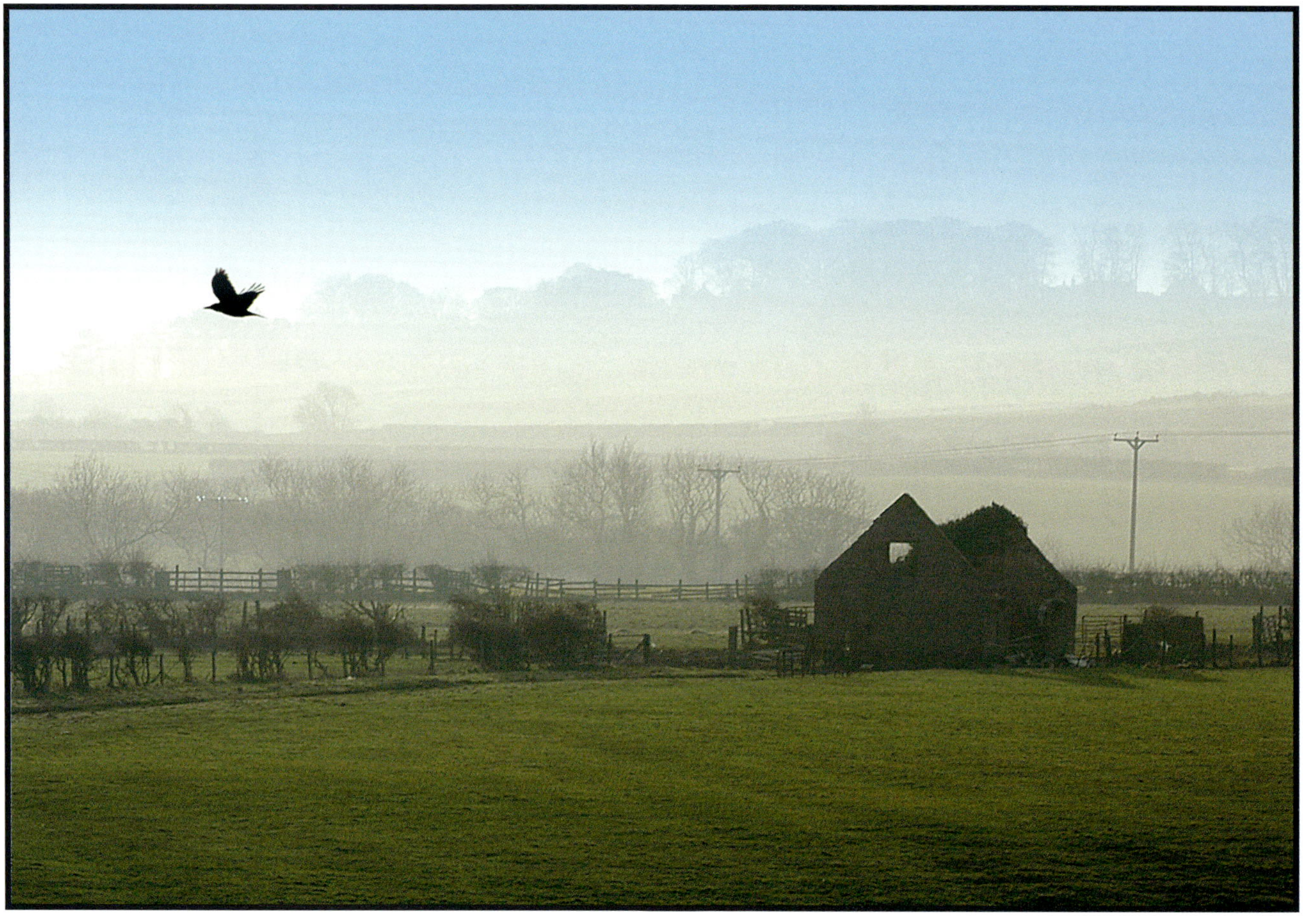

‘As the crow flies’

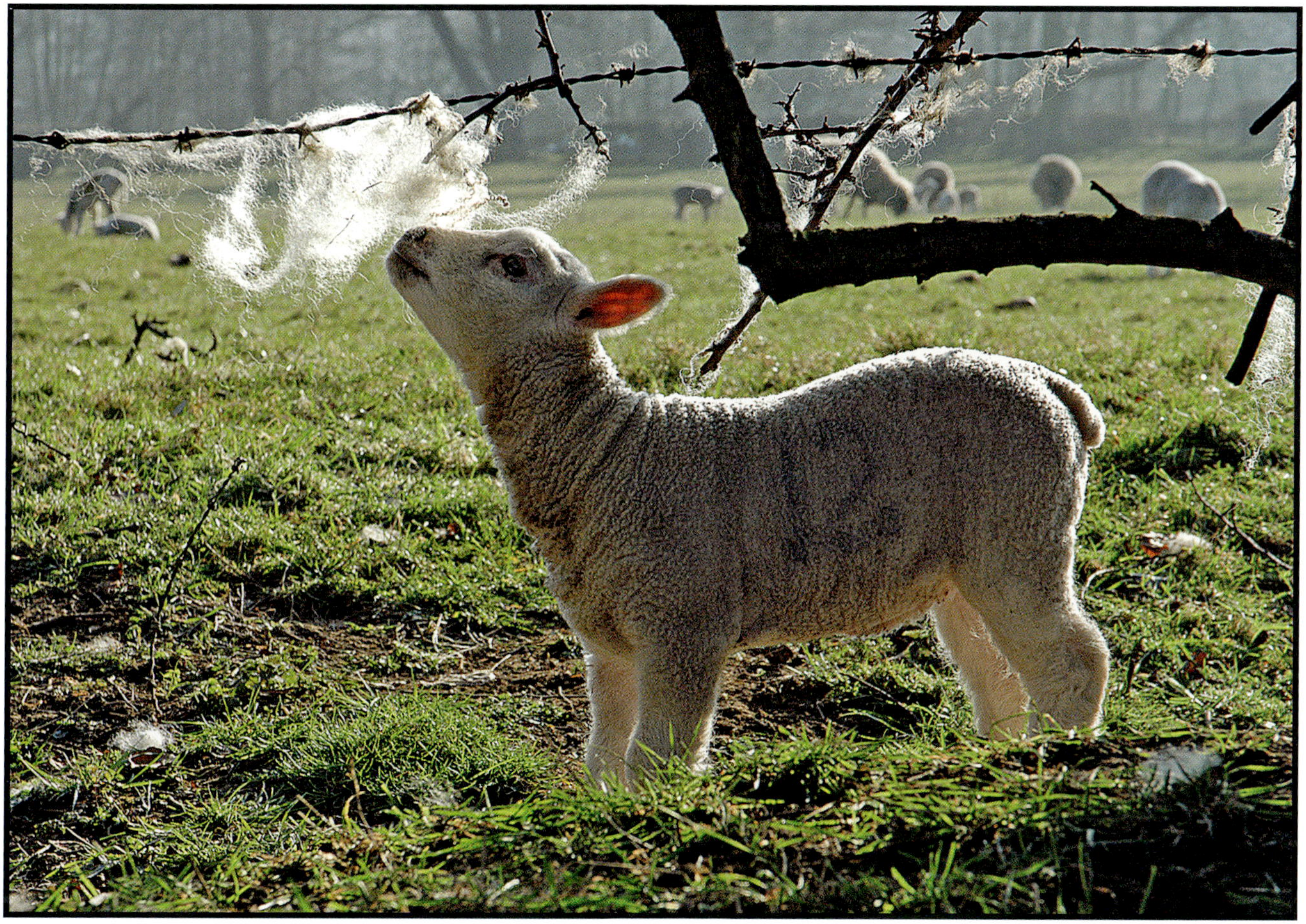

'Pure New Wool'

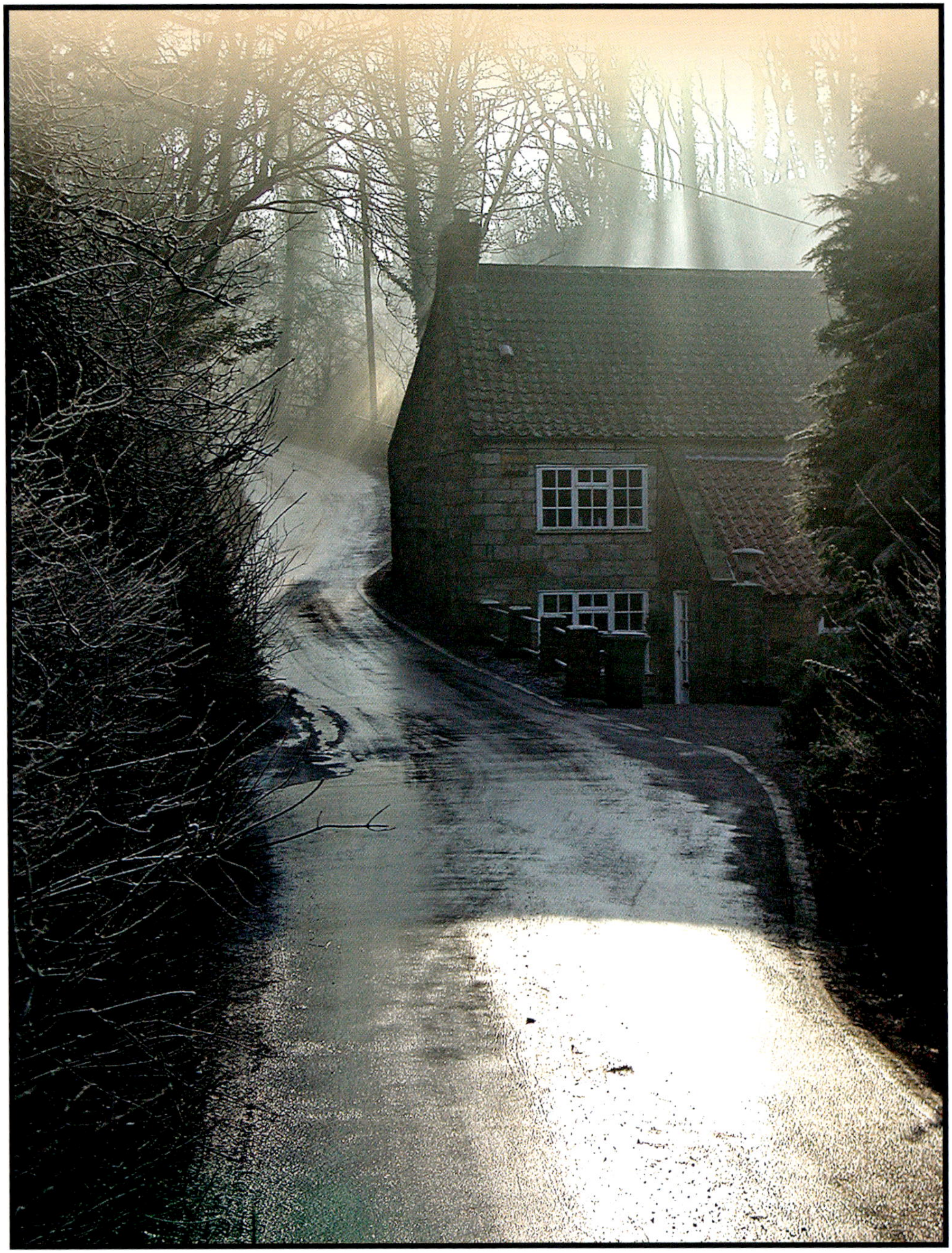

‘Early morning frost, Glen Esk’

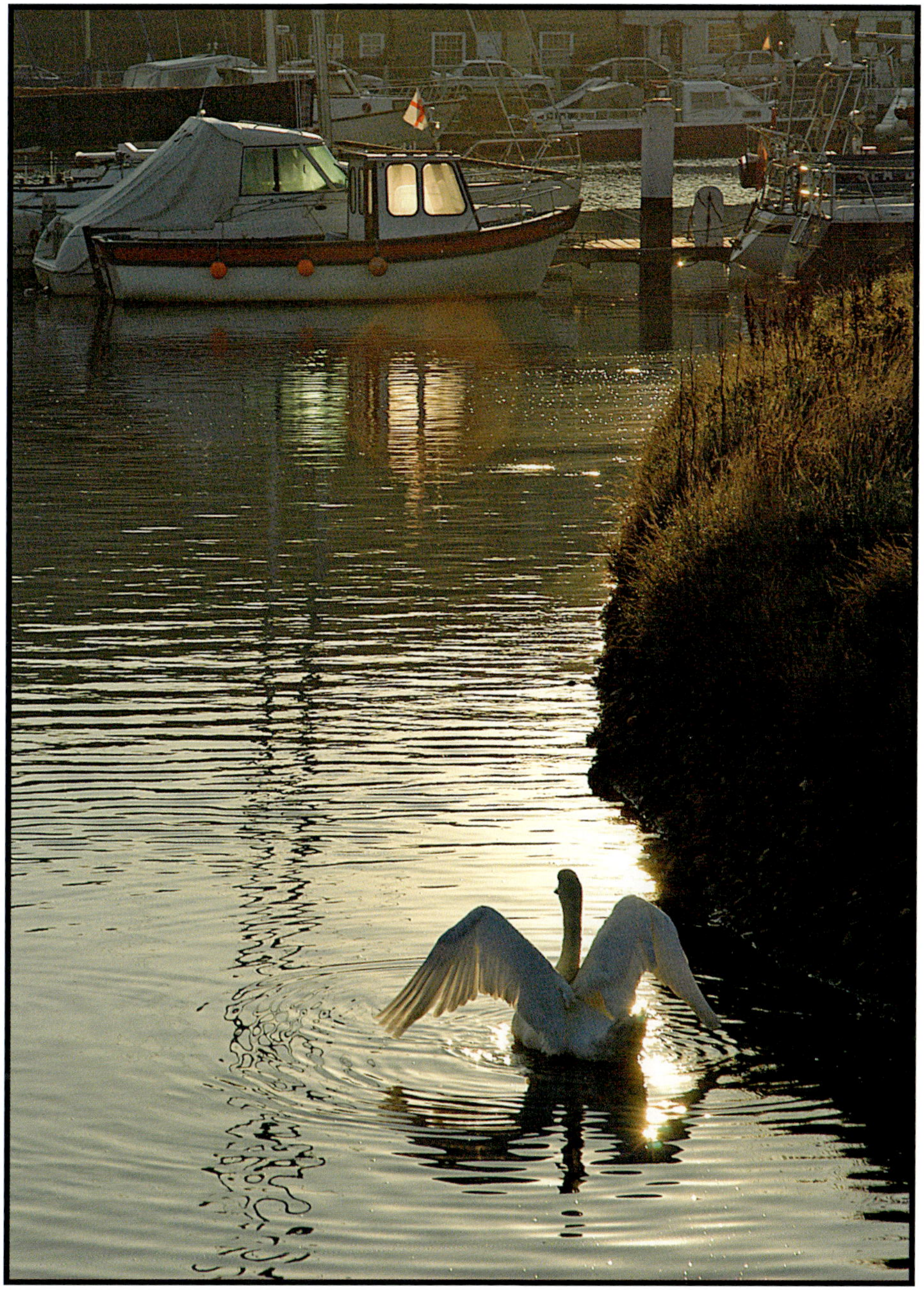

'Spread your wings'

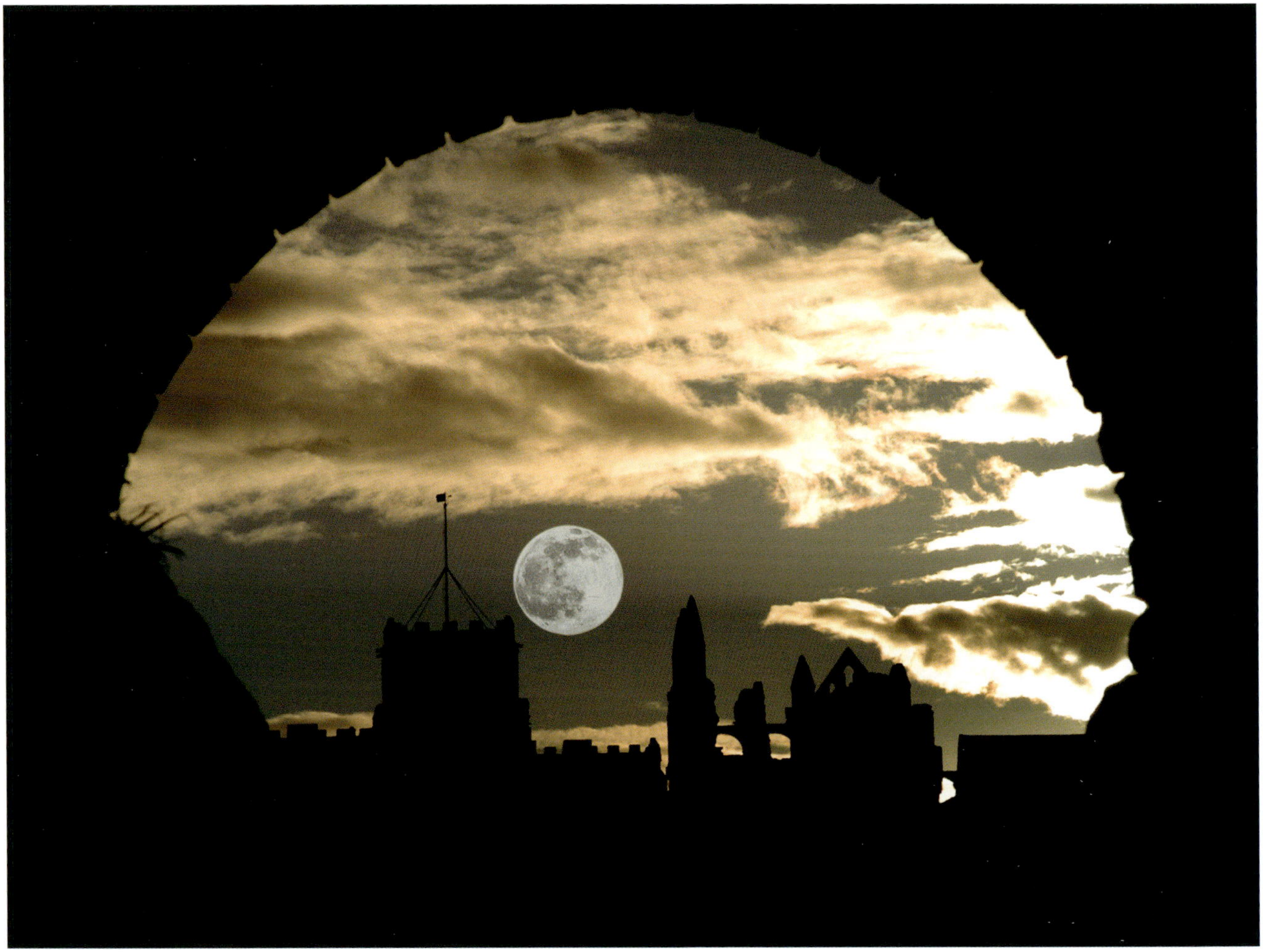

‘Through the keyhole’

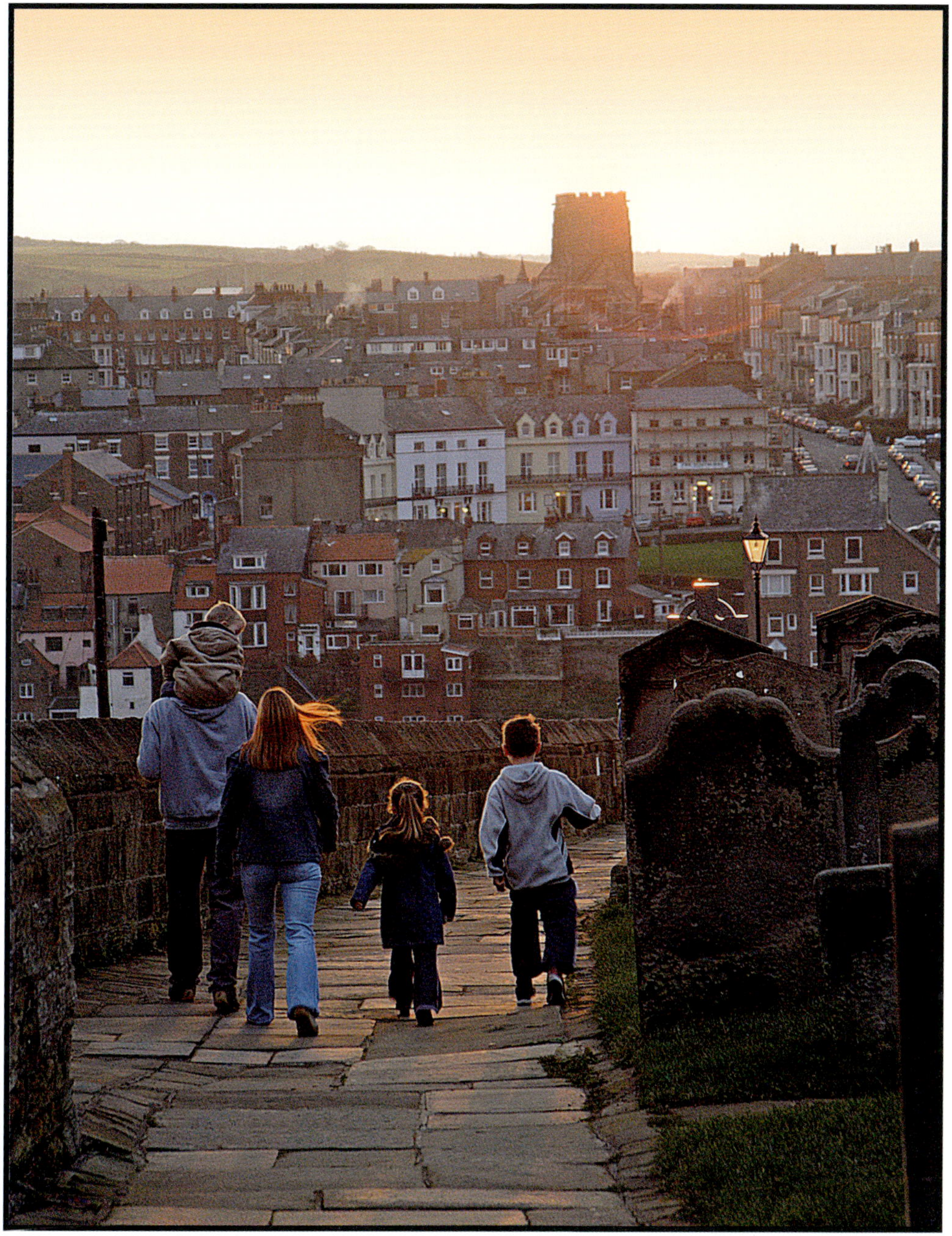

'Top of the 199 steps'

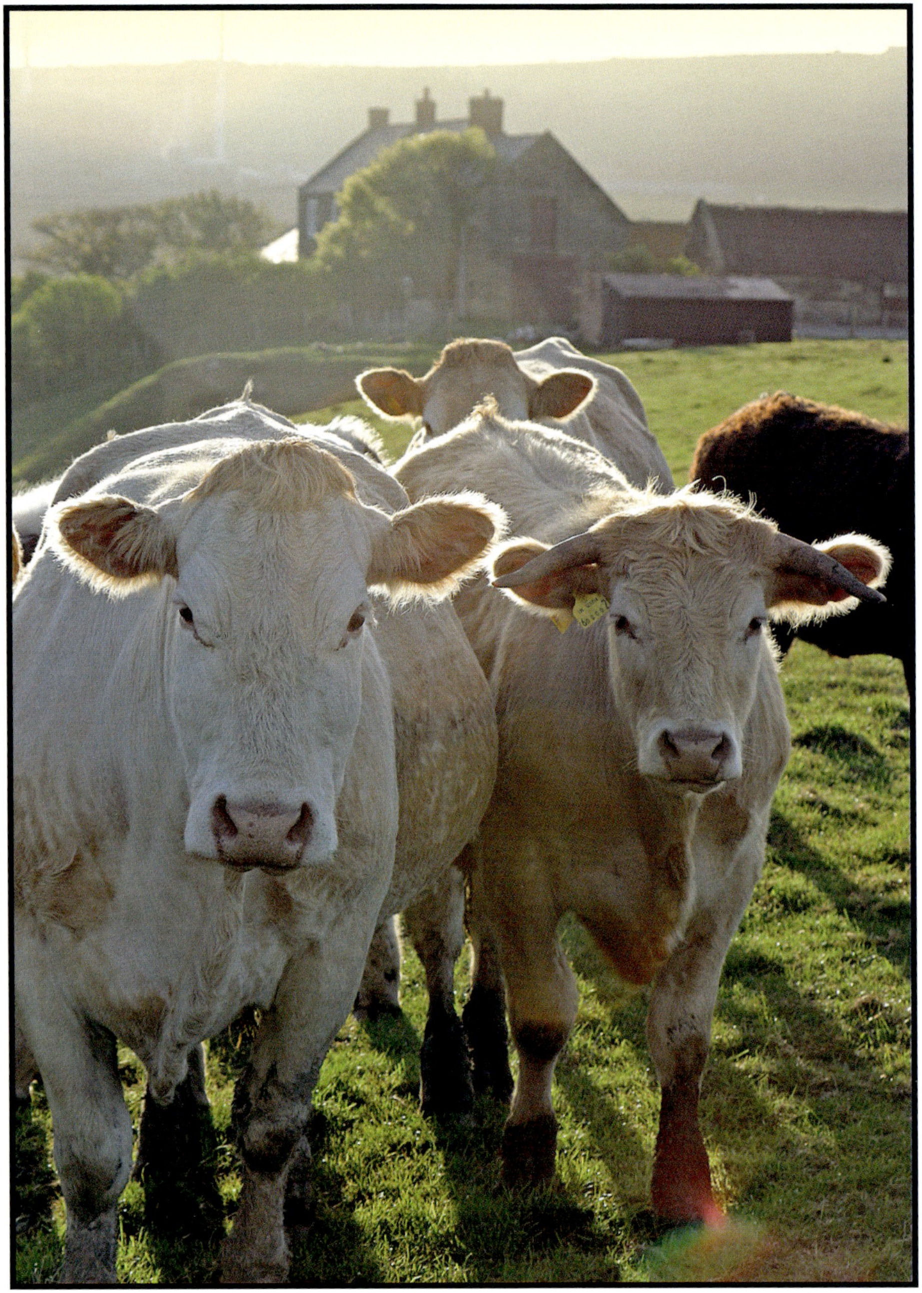

‘Herd the news?’

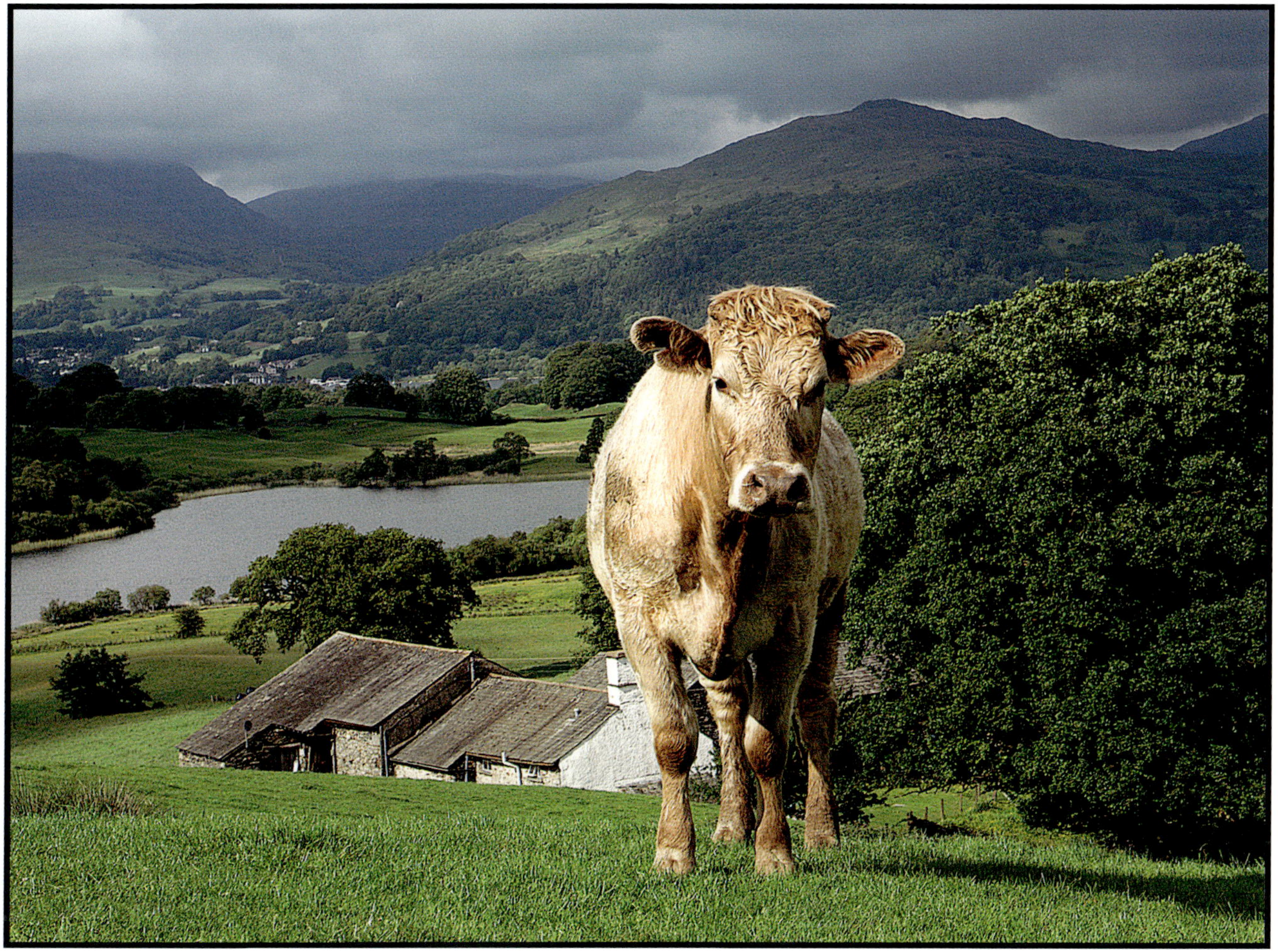

'Curious cow'

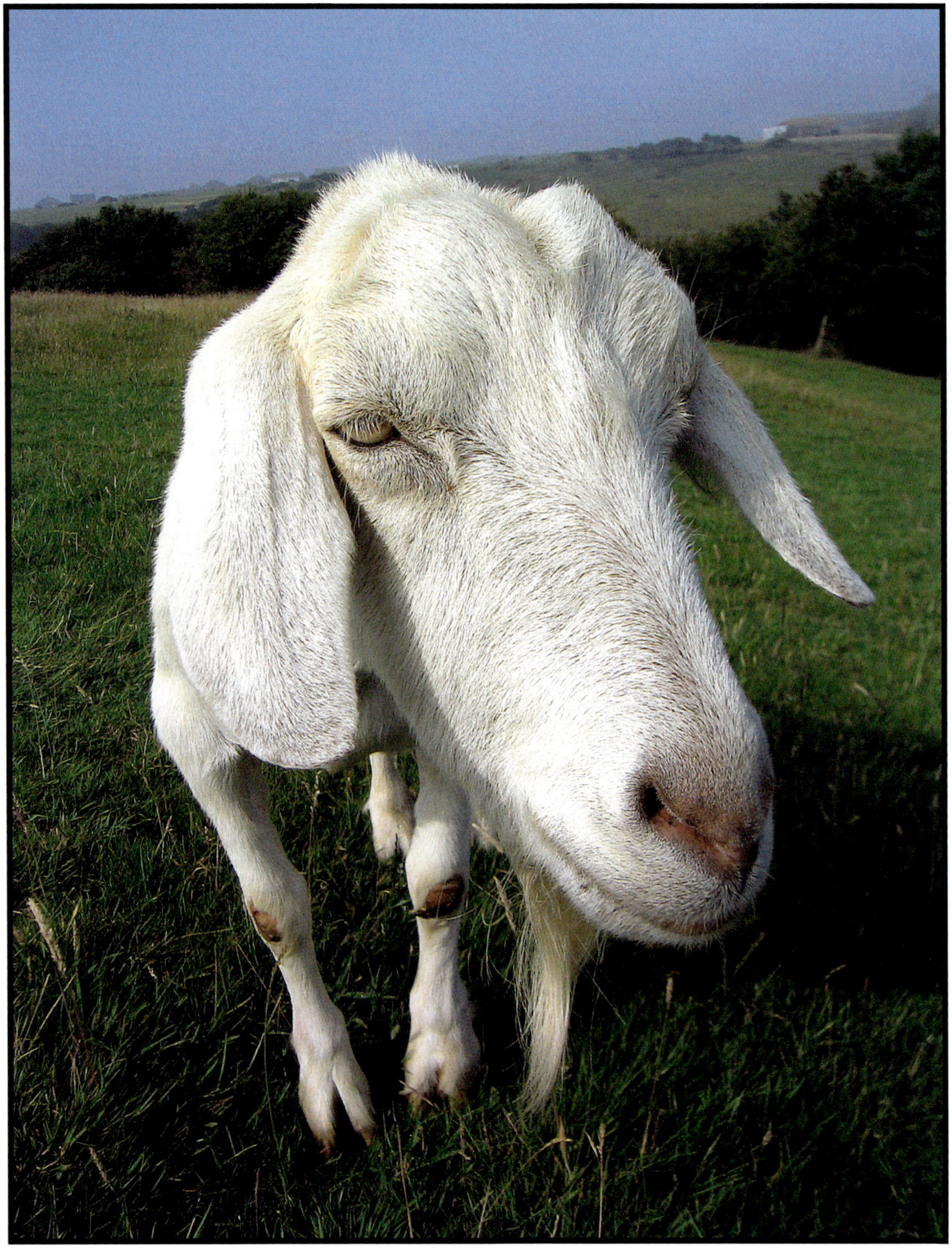

‘Old goat’

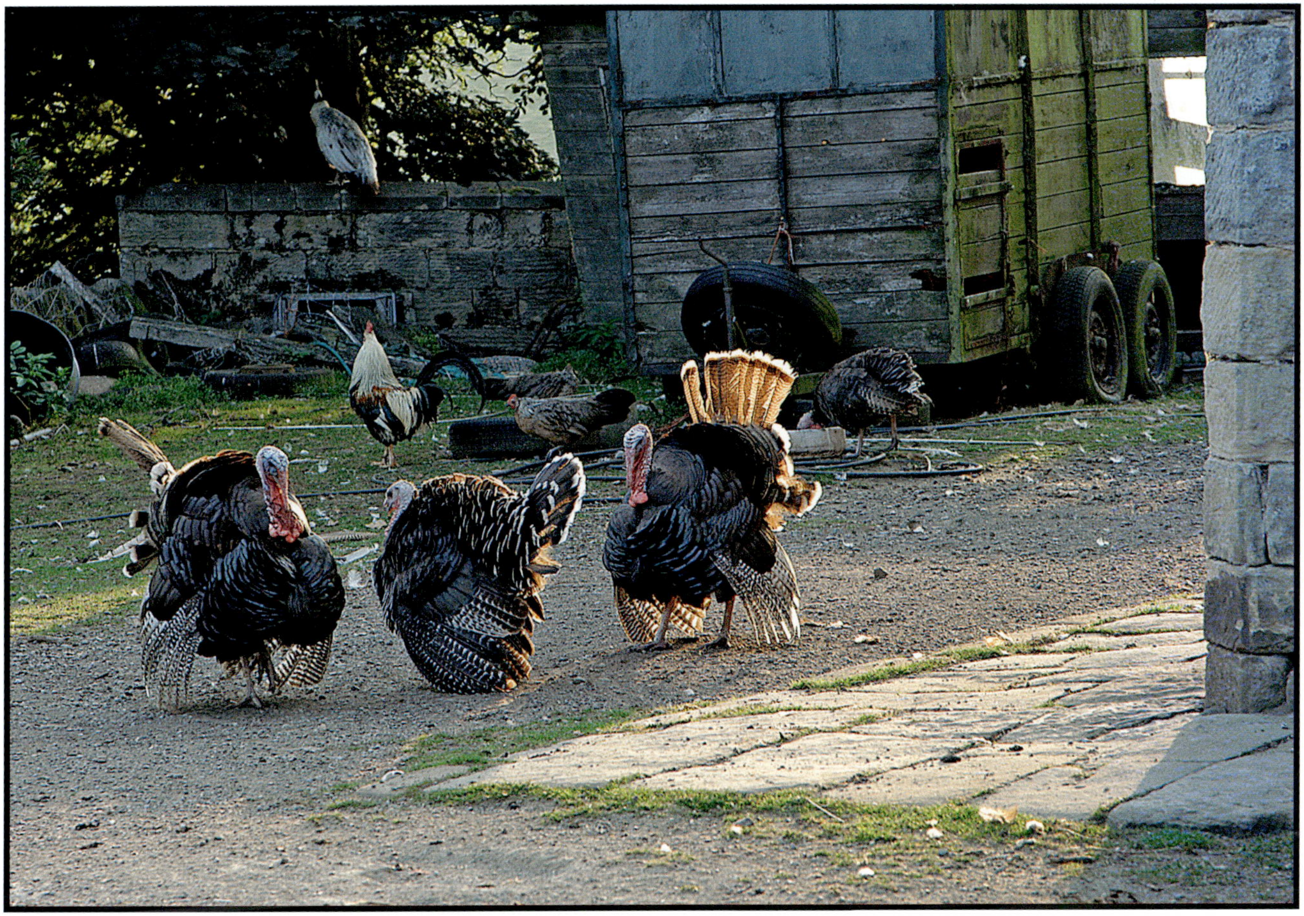

'Fowl play'

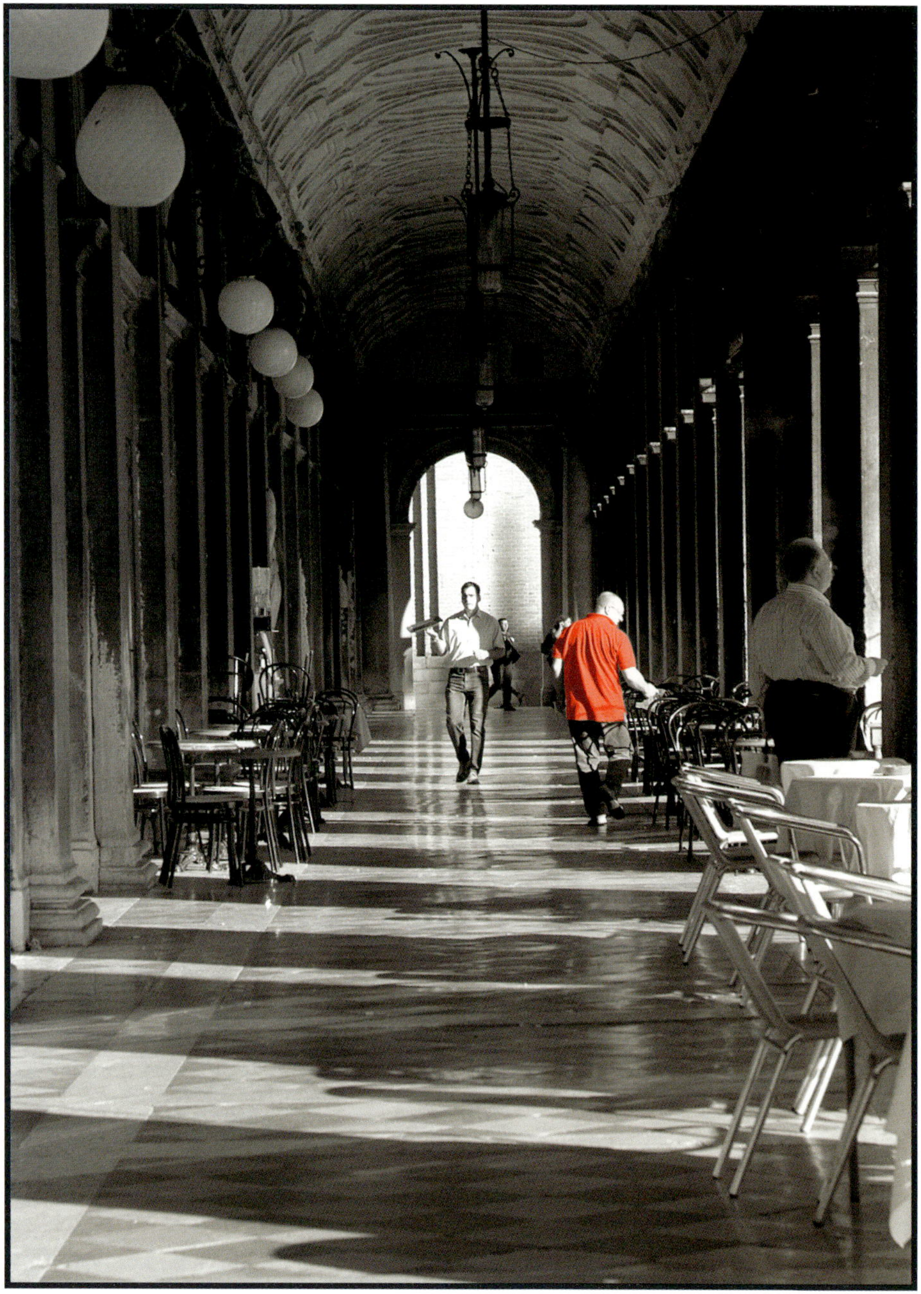

‘Venetian arcade’

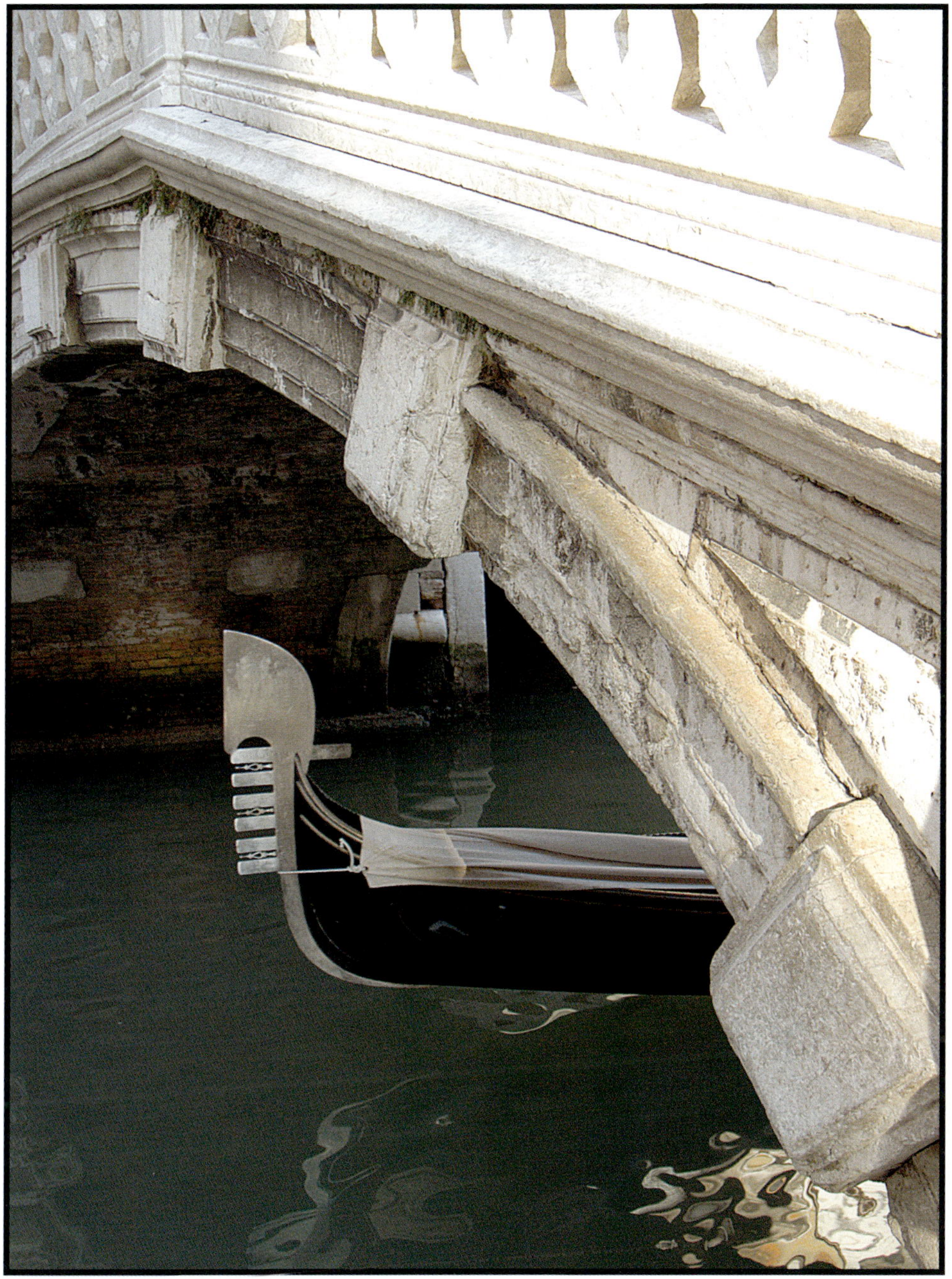

‘Under the marble bridge’

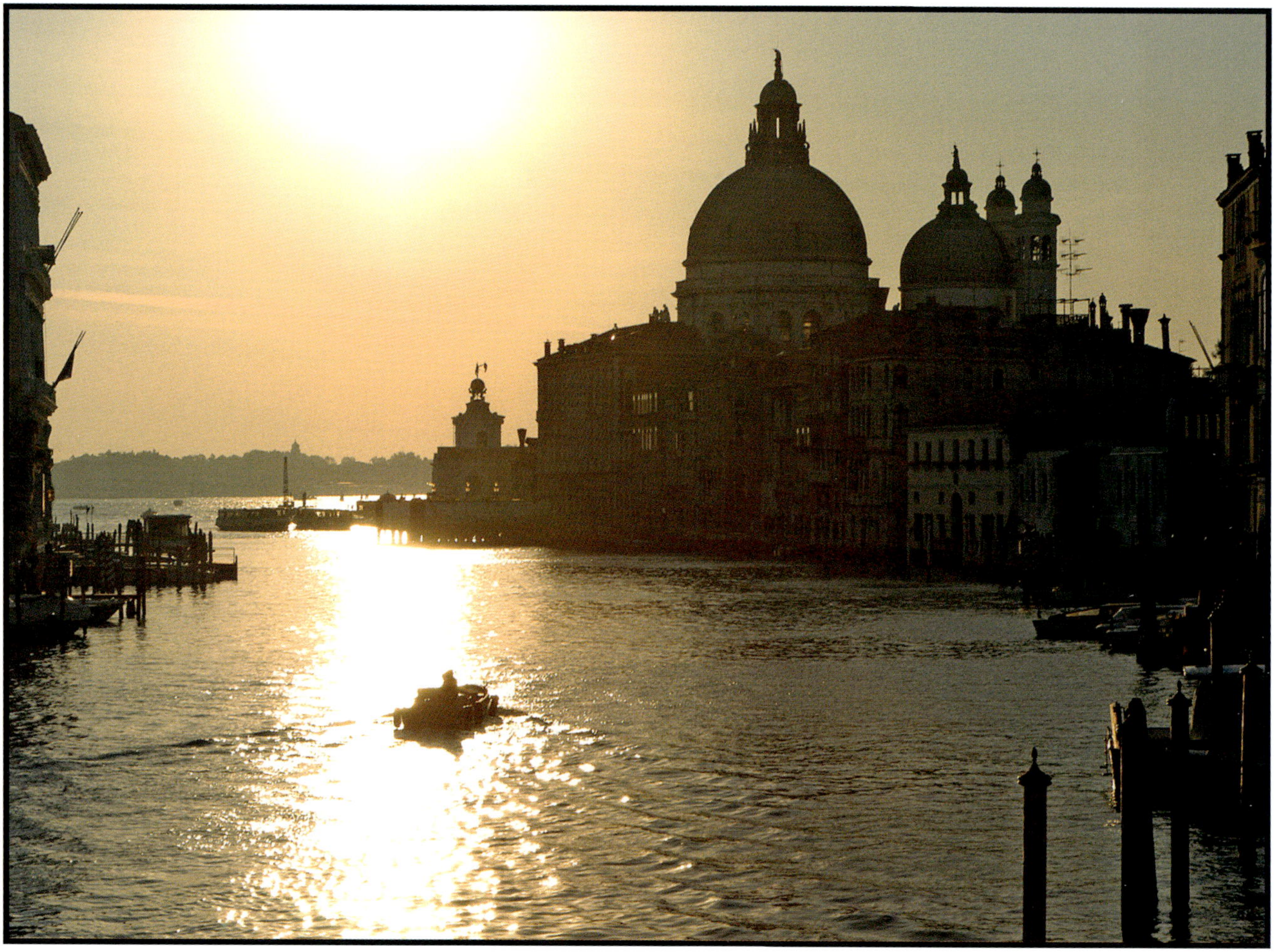

‘Grand Canal, Venice’

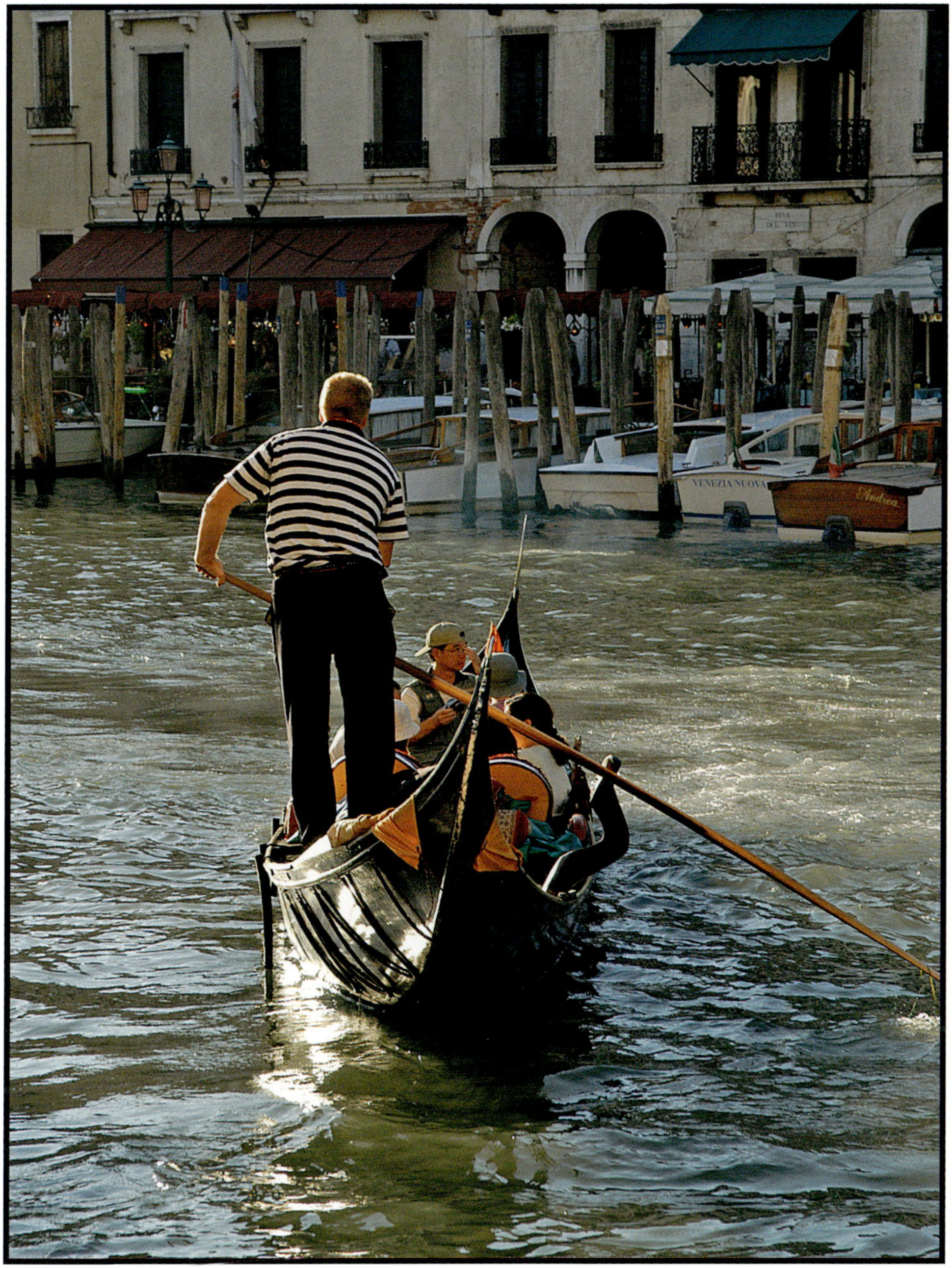

'The Gondolier'

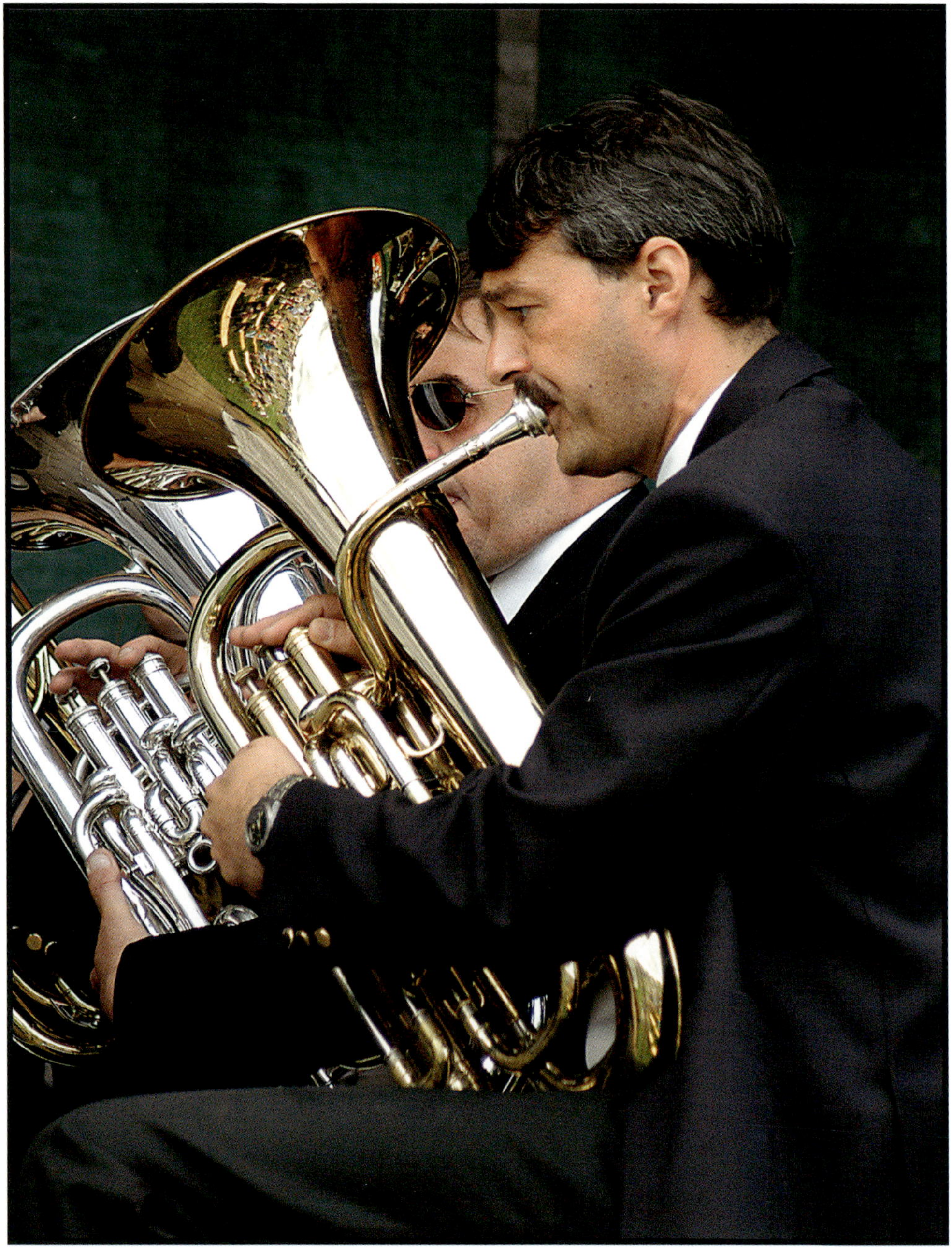

‘Brass band, Egton show’

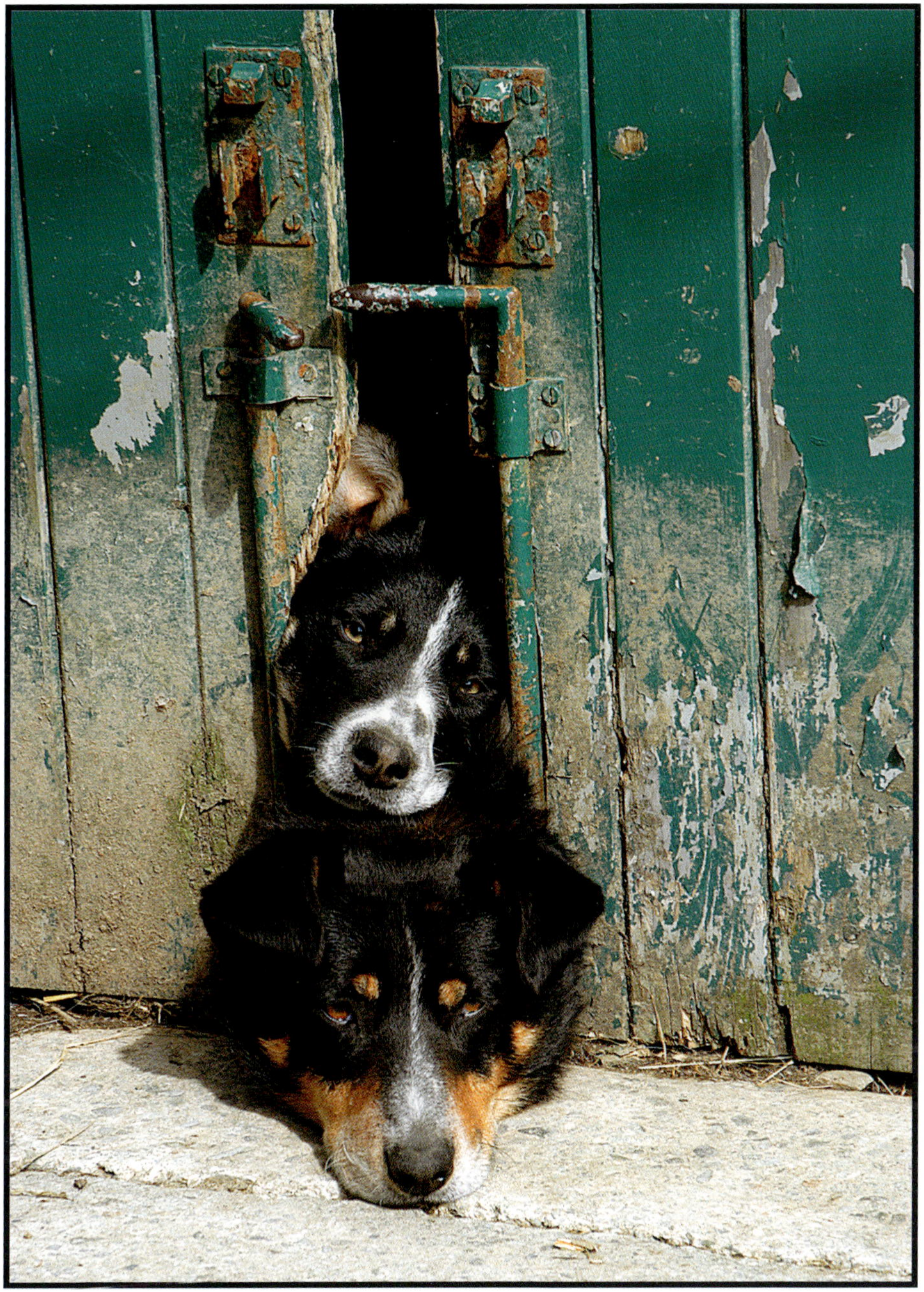

'Top dog'

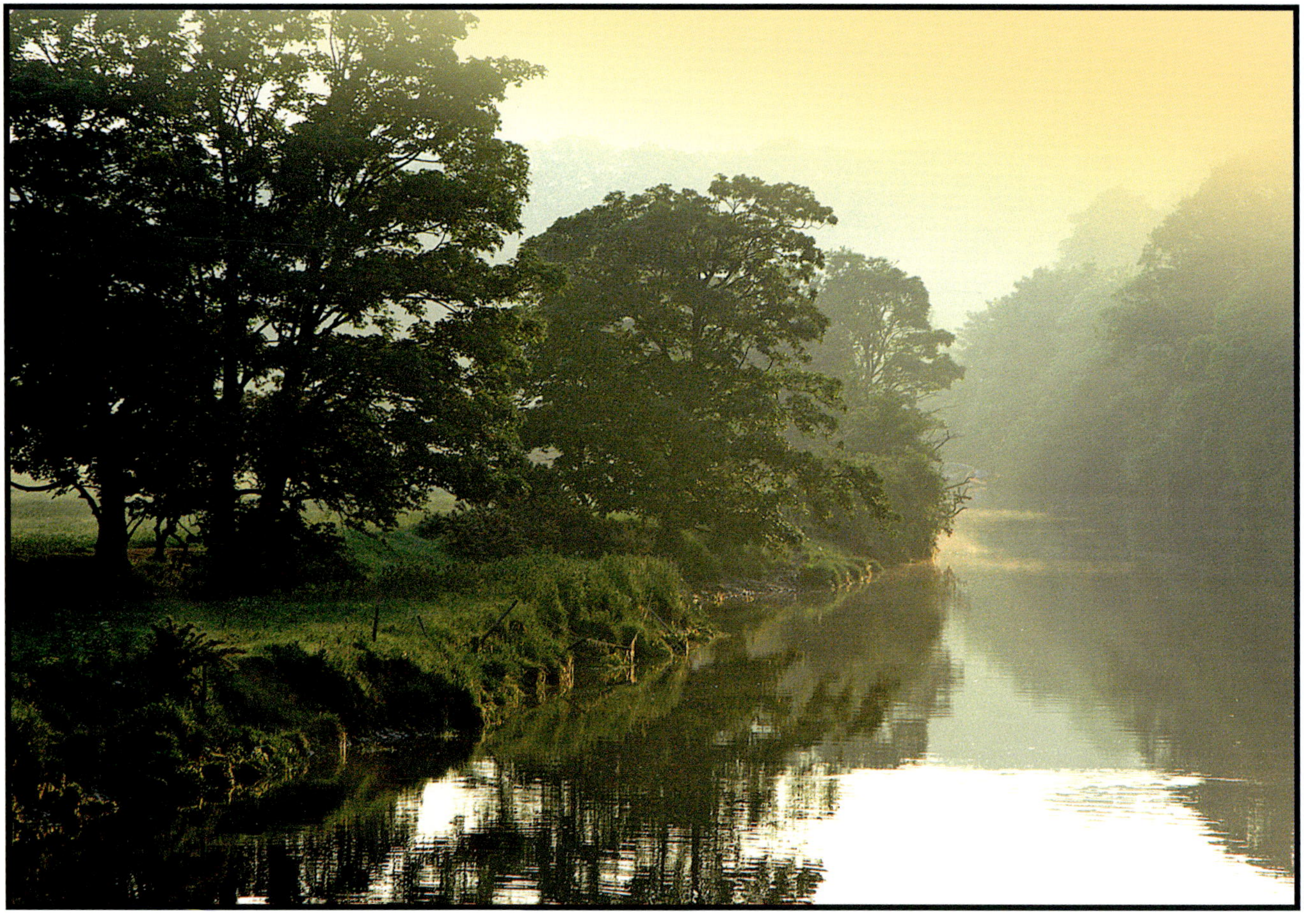

'A new dawn'

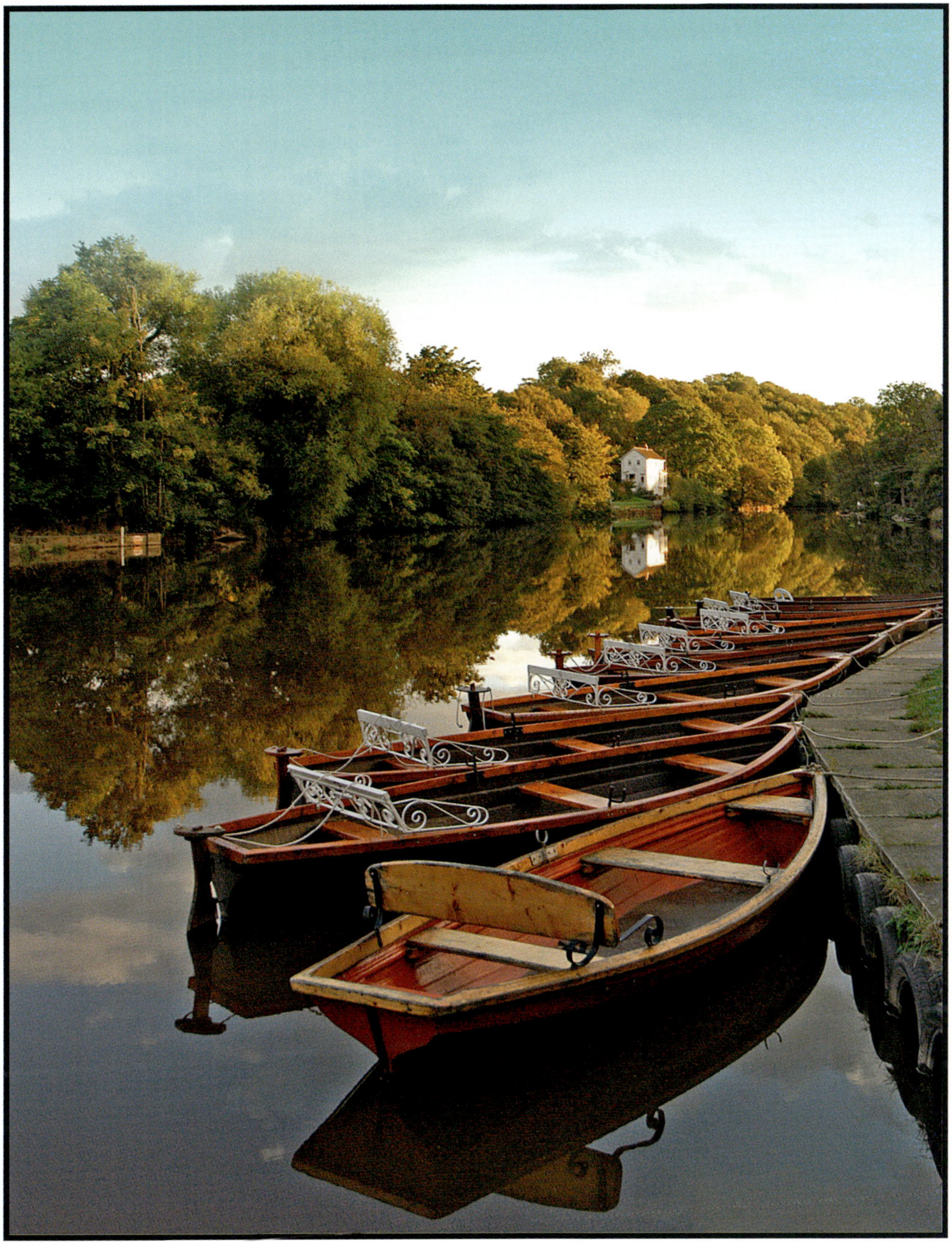

'On reflection...'

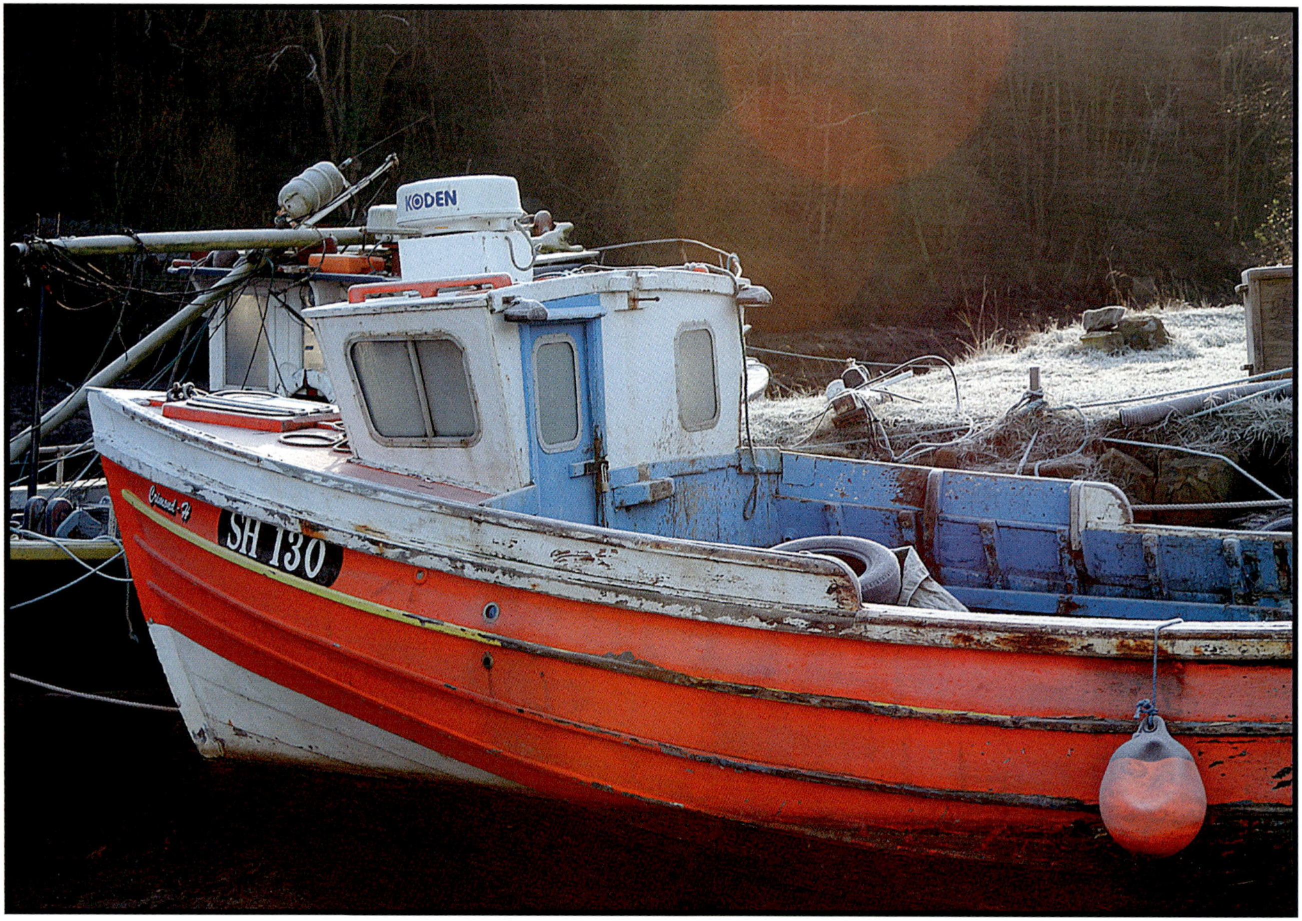

'Red lipstick on the old girl'

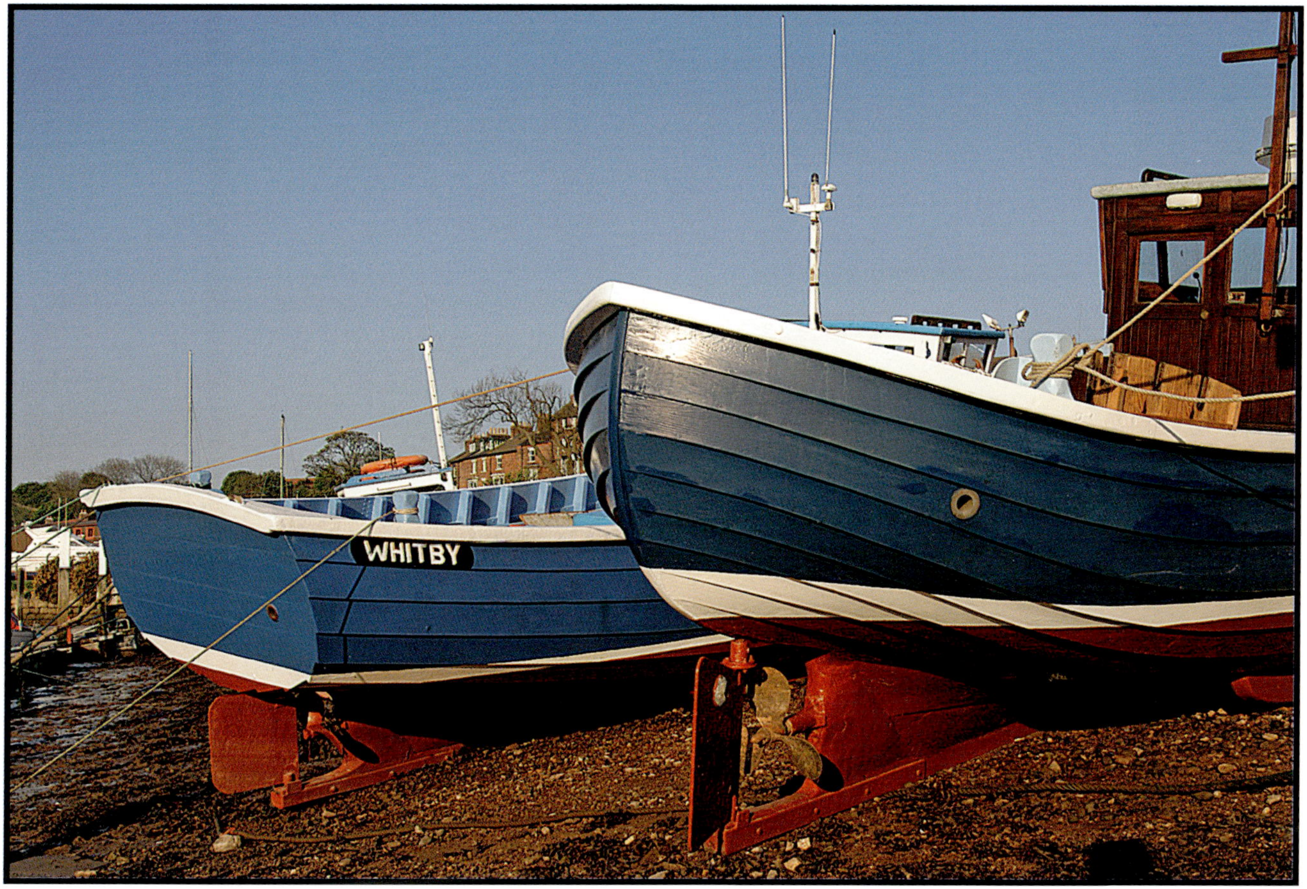

'Blue boats, Whitby marina'

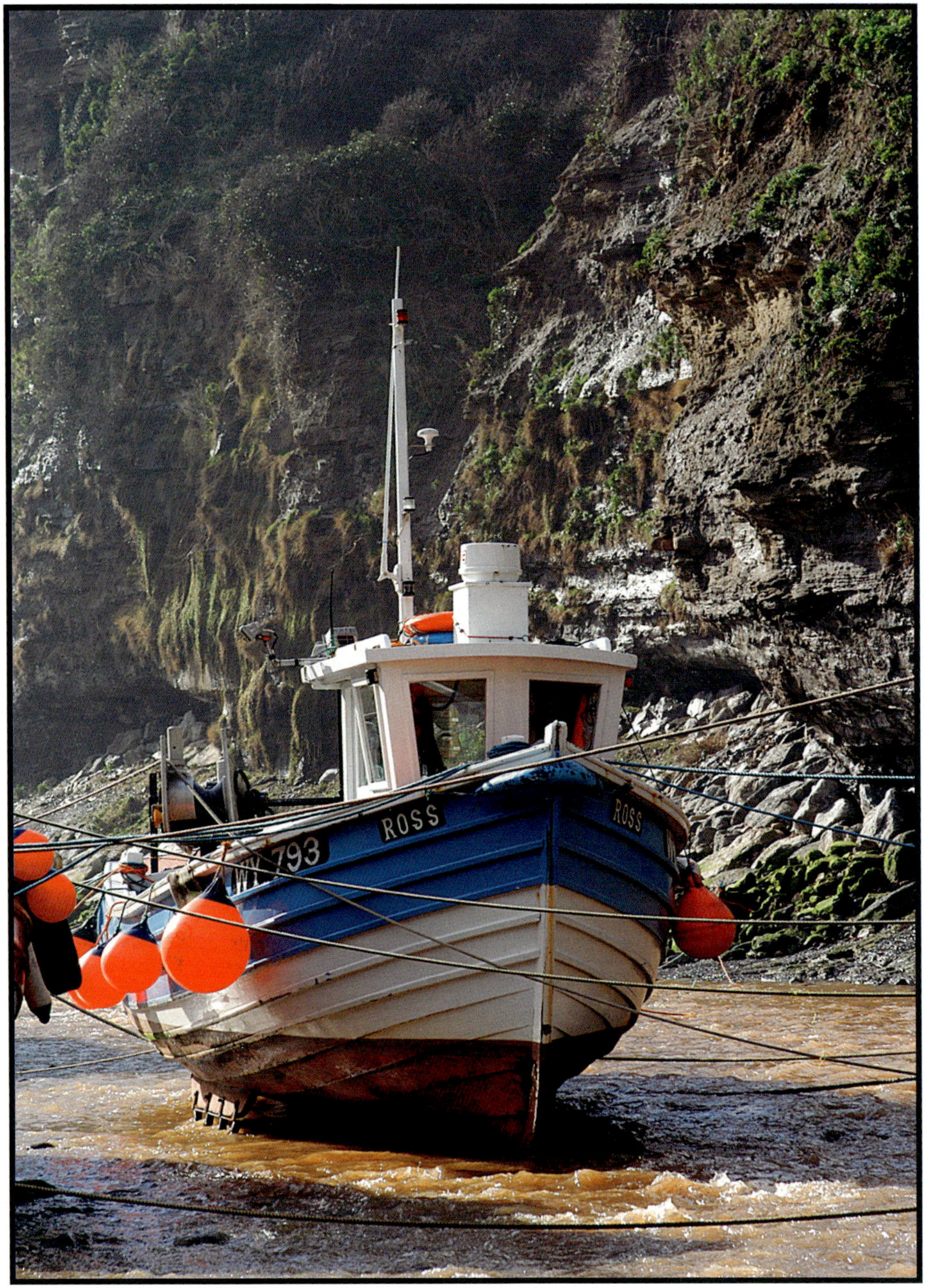

'Staithes beck'

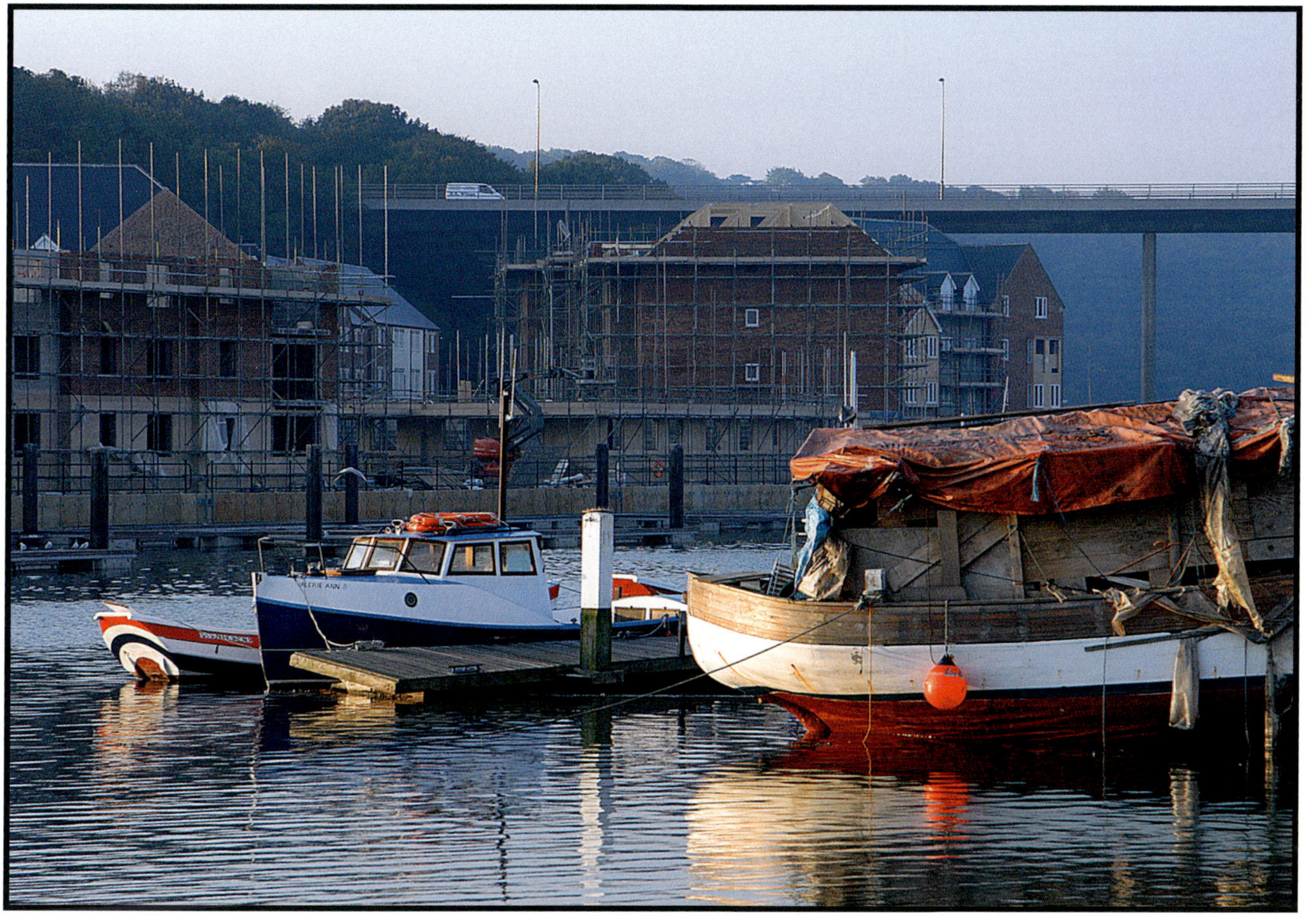

'Whitehall landing'

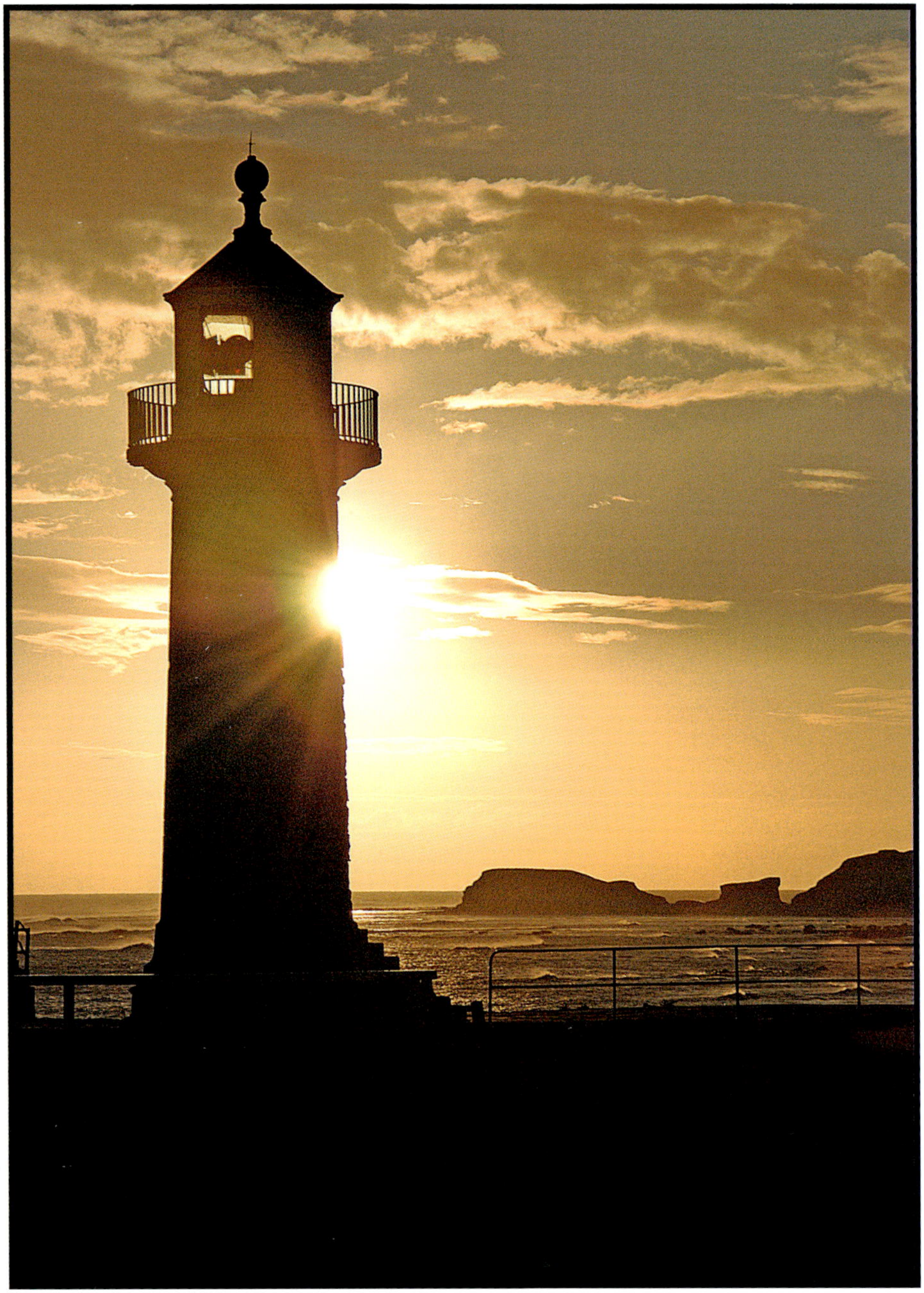

‘Sunrise’

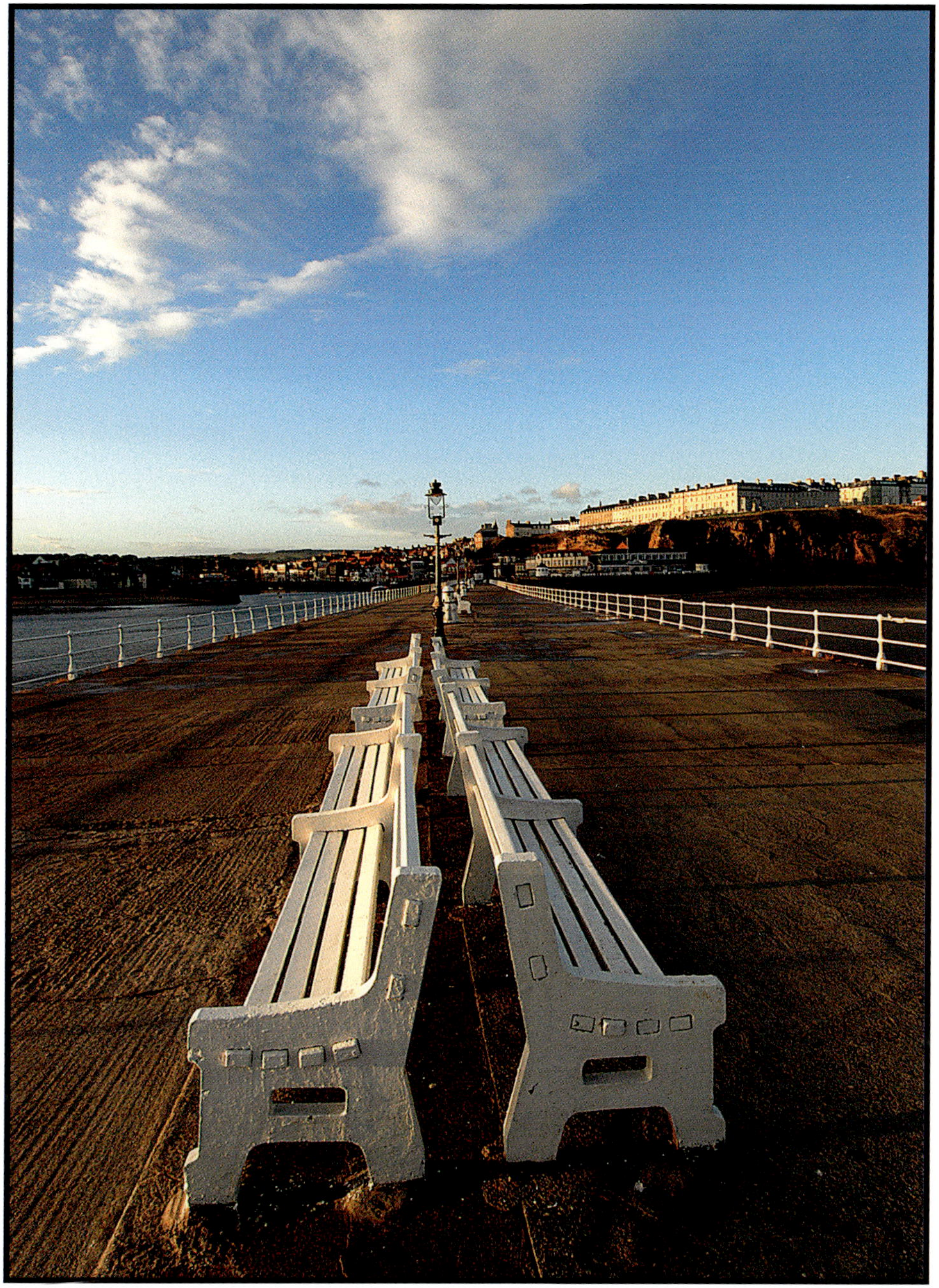

'West pier, Whitby'

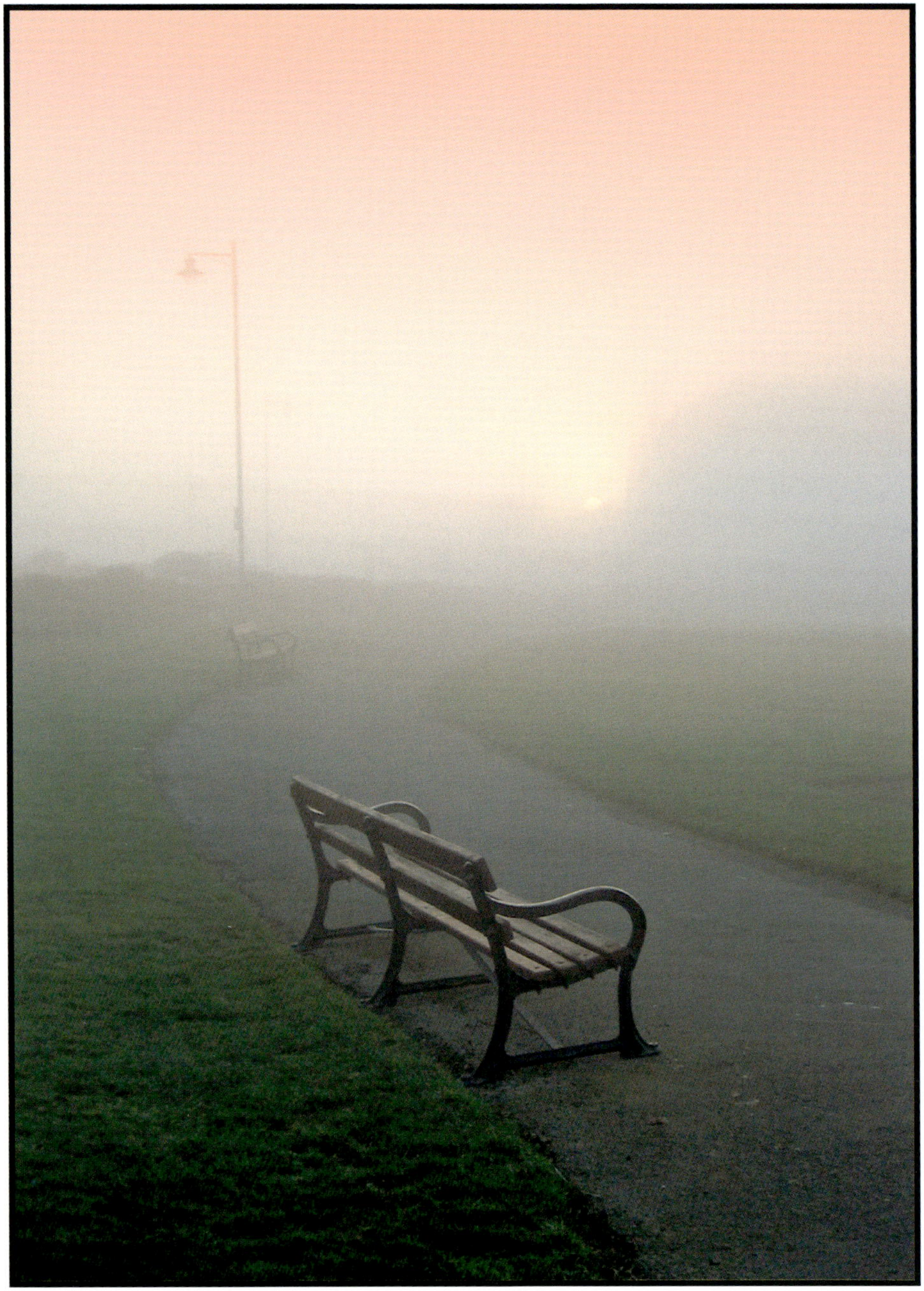

‘Misty sunset’

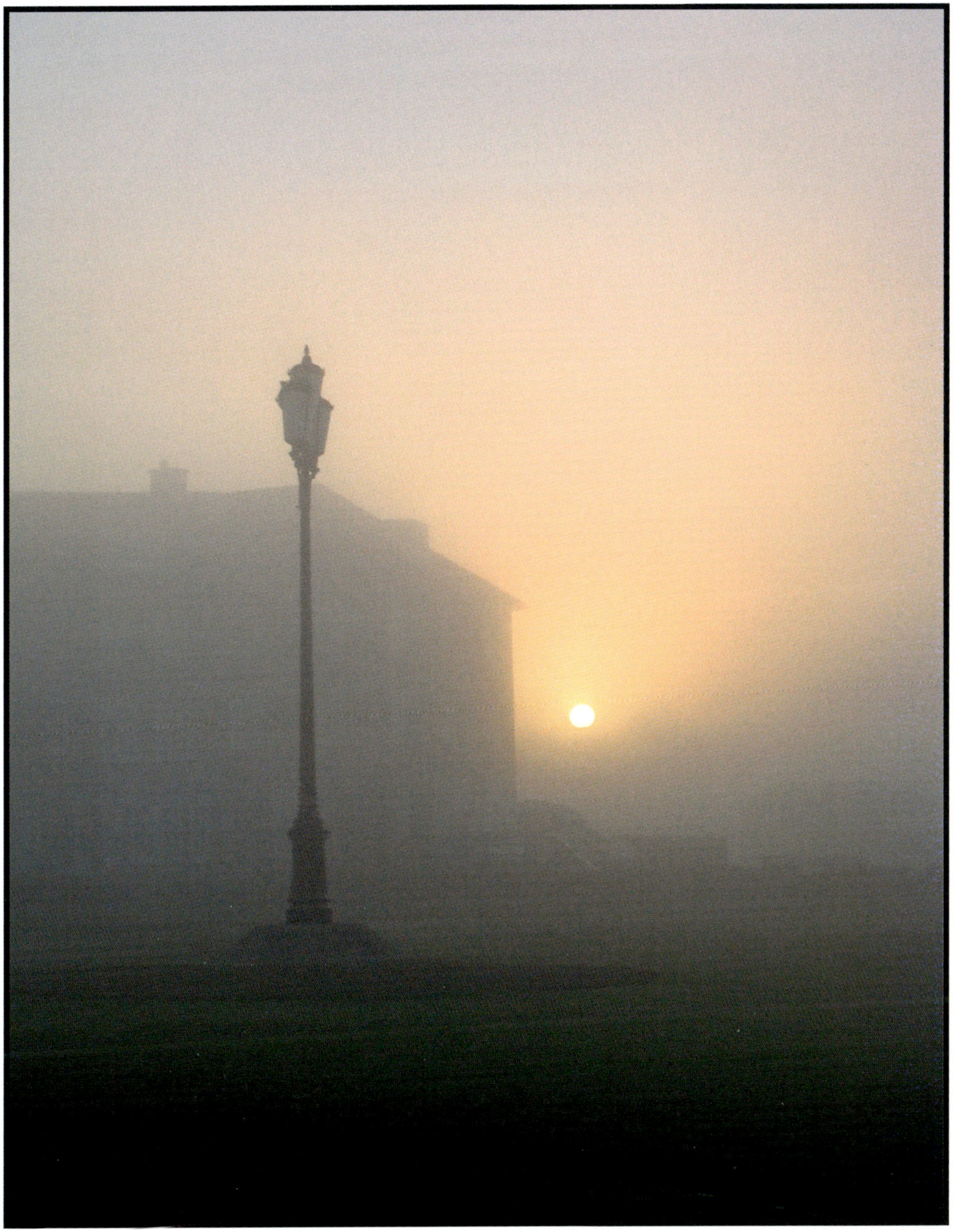

‘Crescent gardens, Whitby’

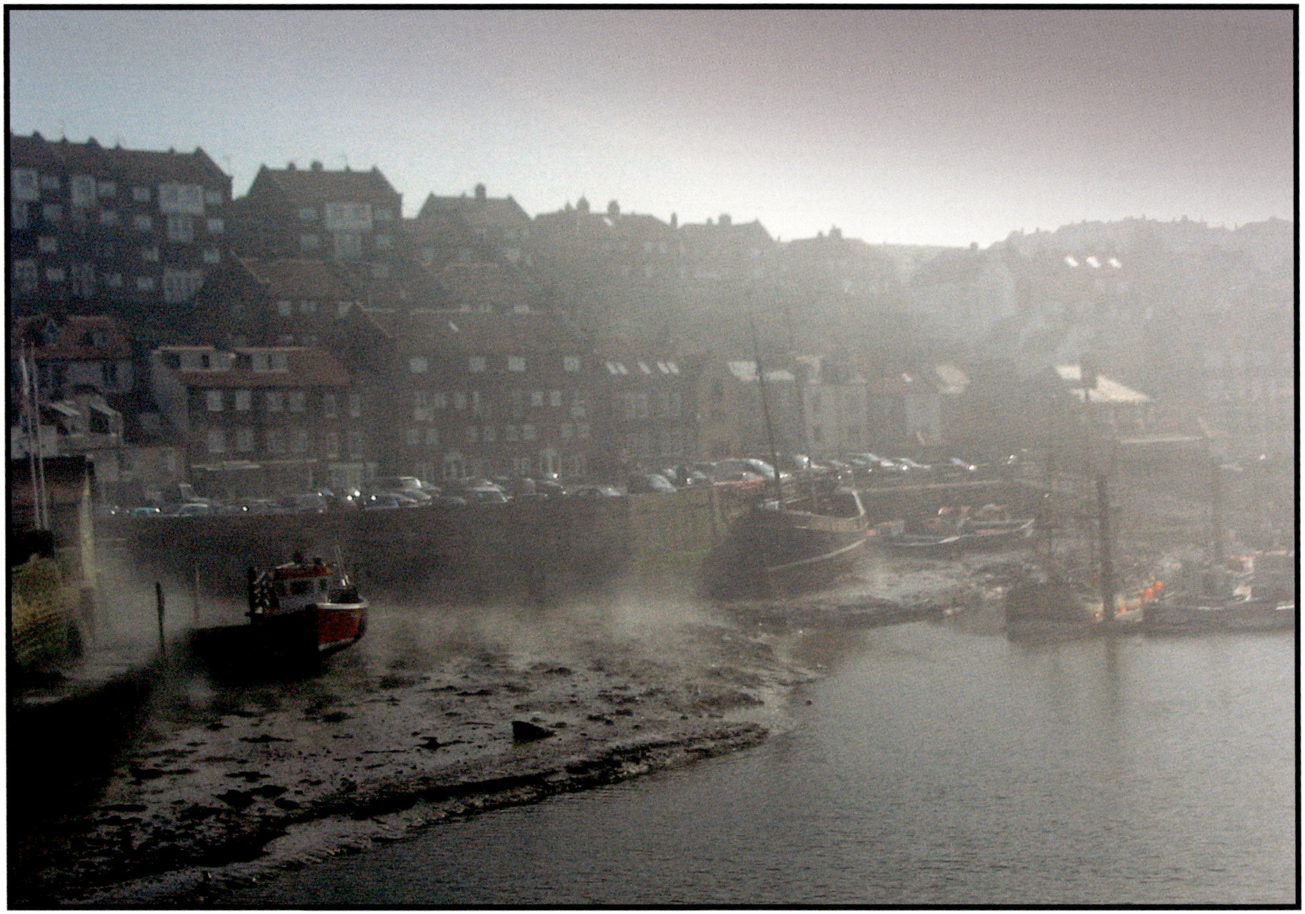

‘Misty sands’

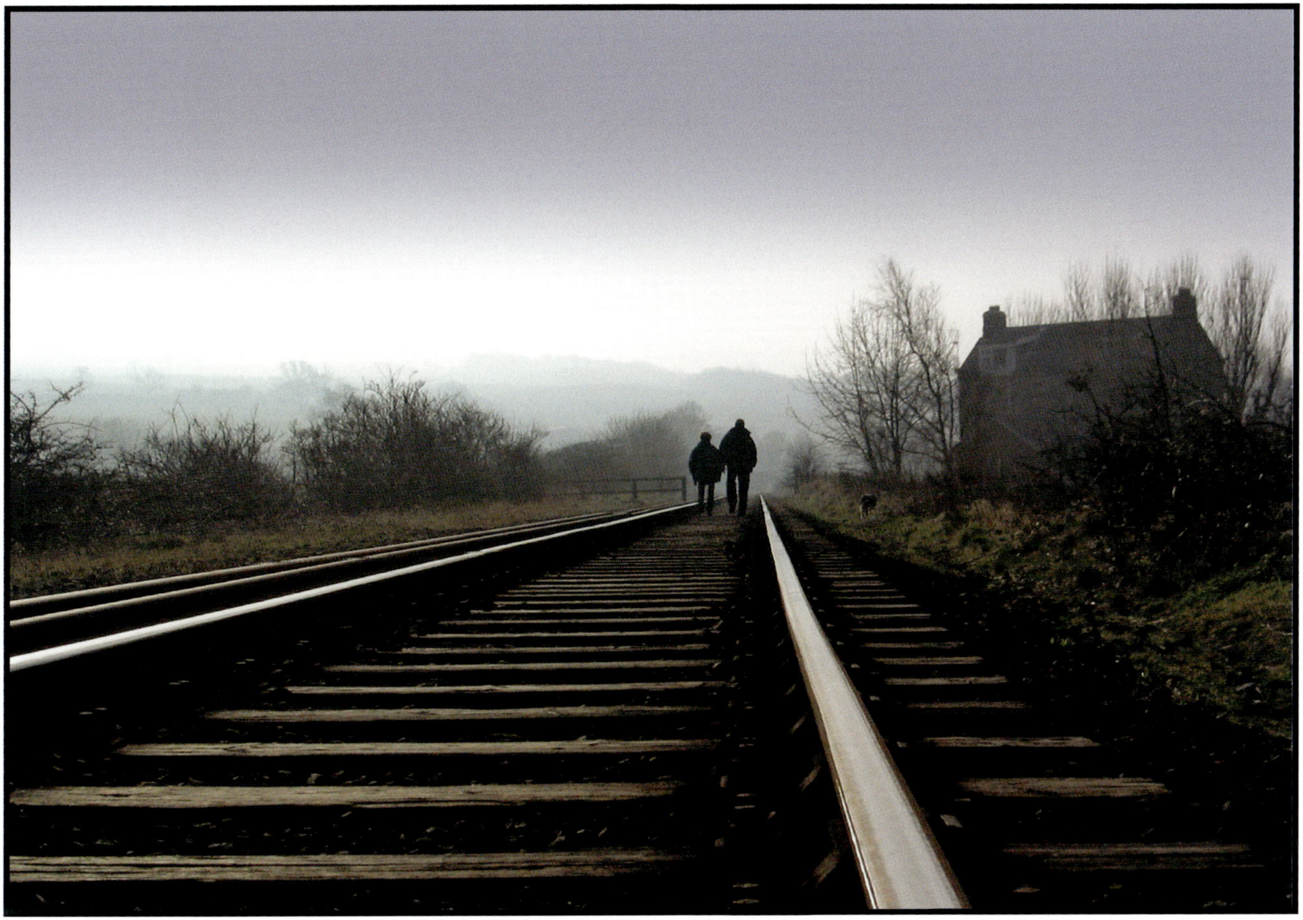

'On the right track'

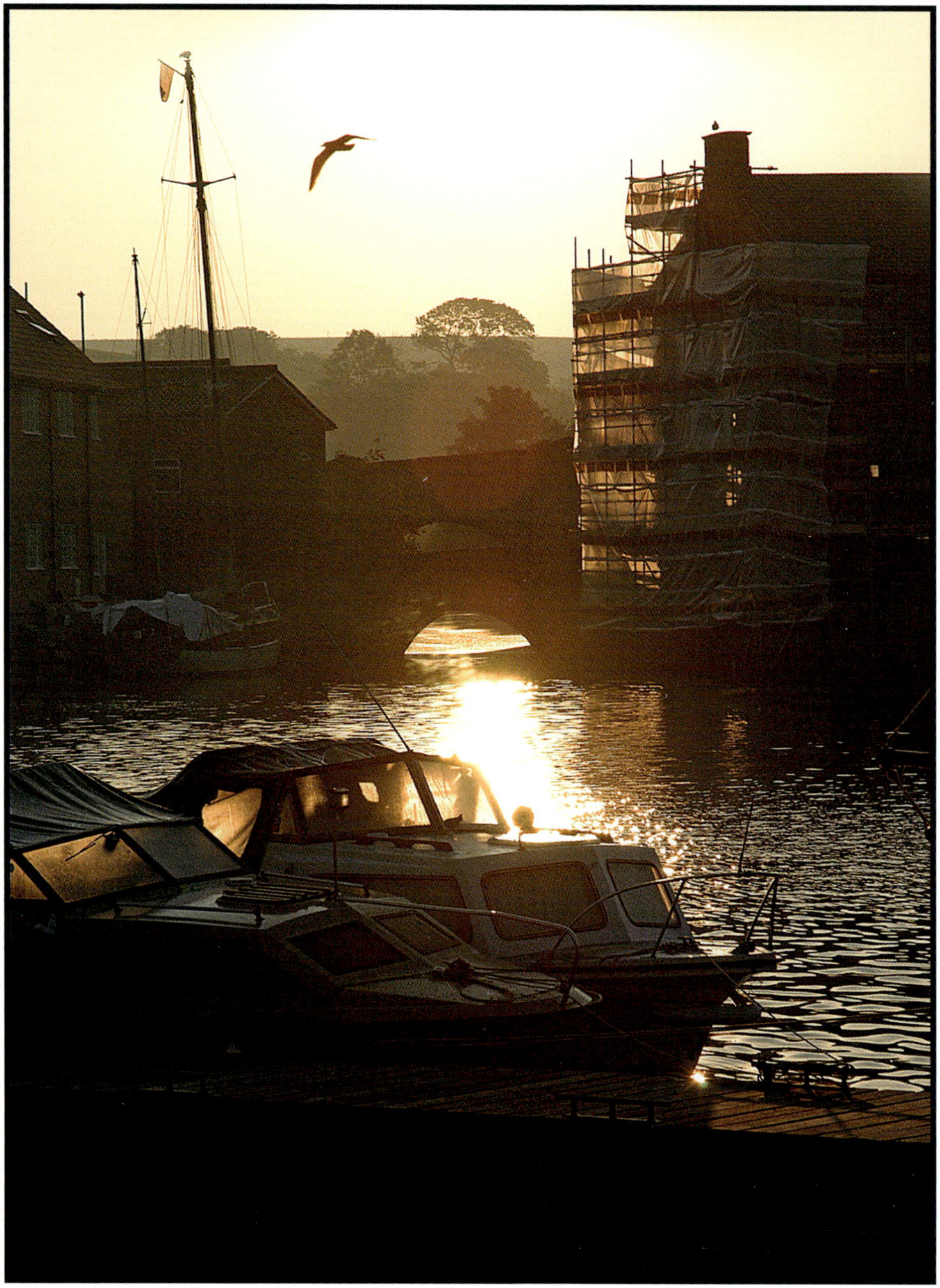

‘Two bridges’

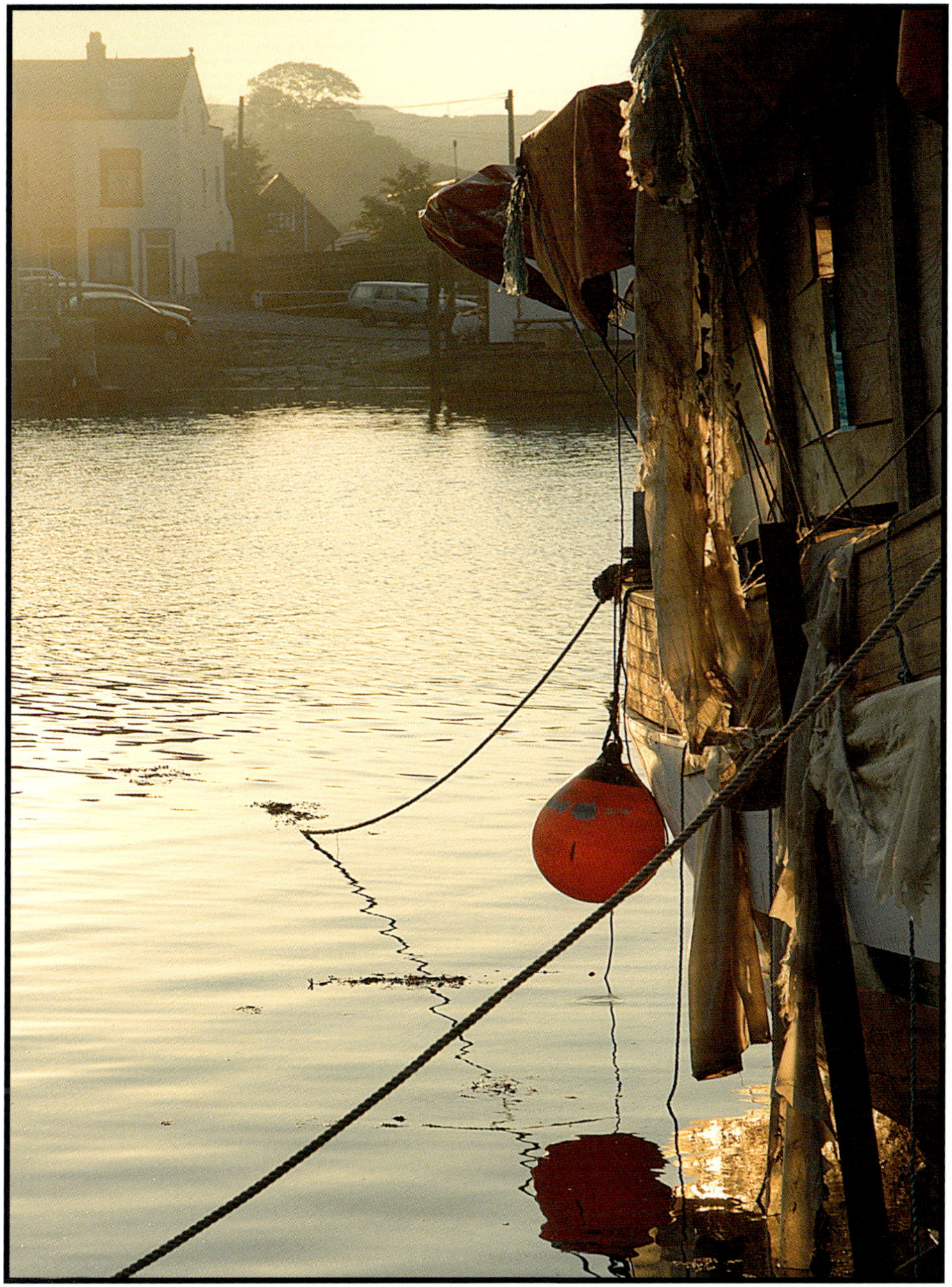

'Warm dawn'

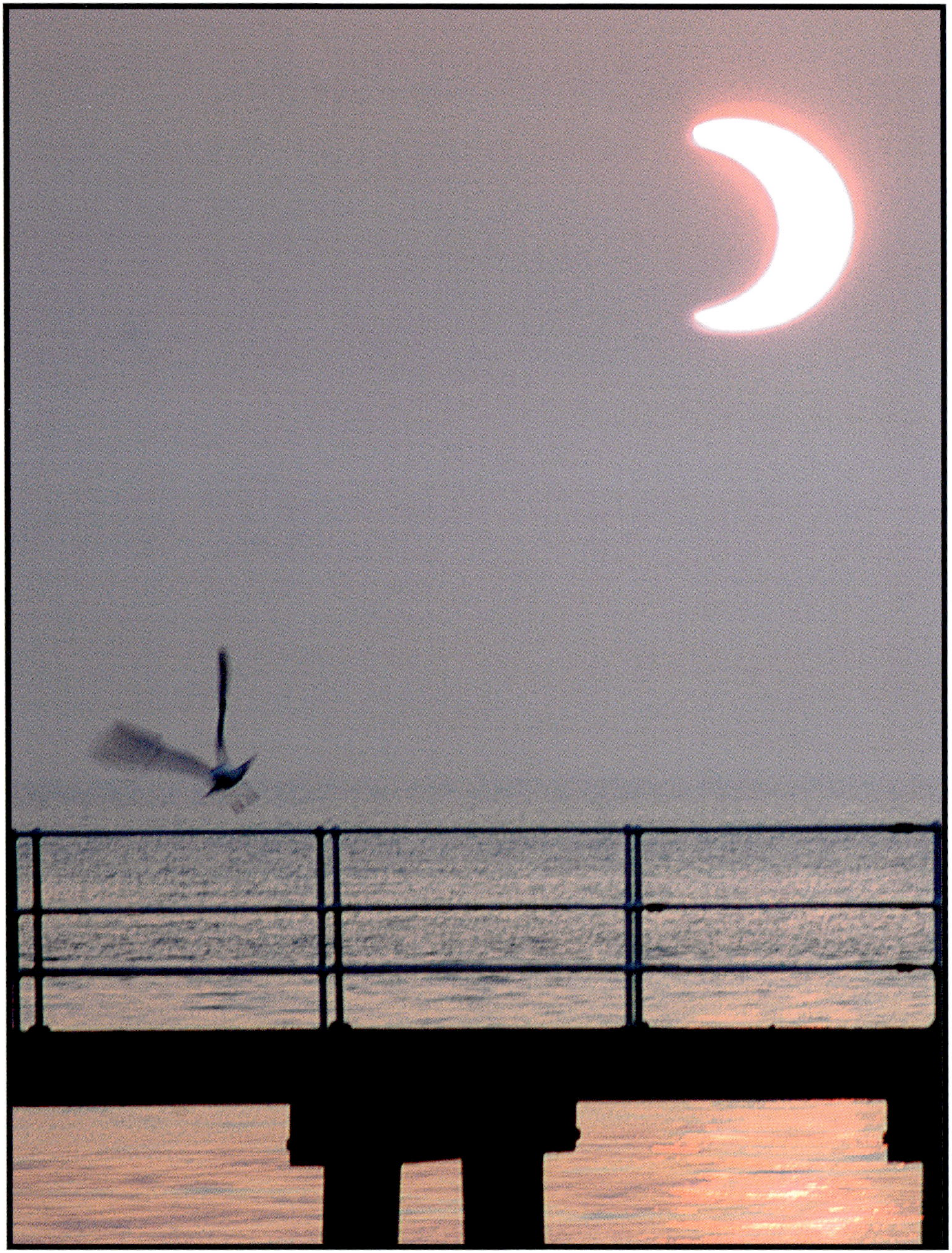

‘Partial eclipse, Whitby’

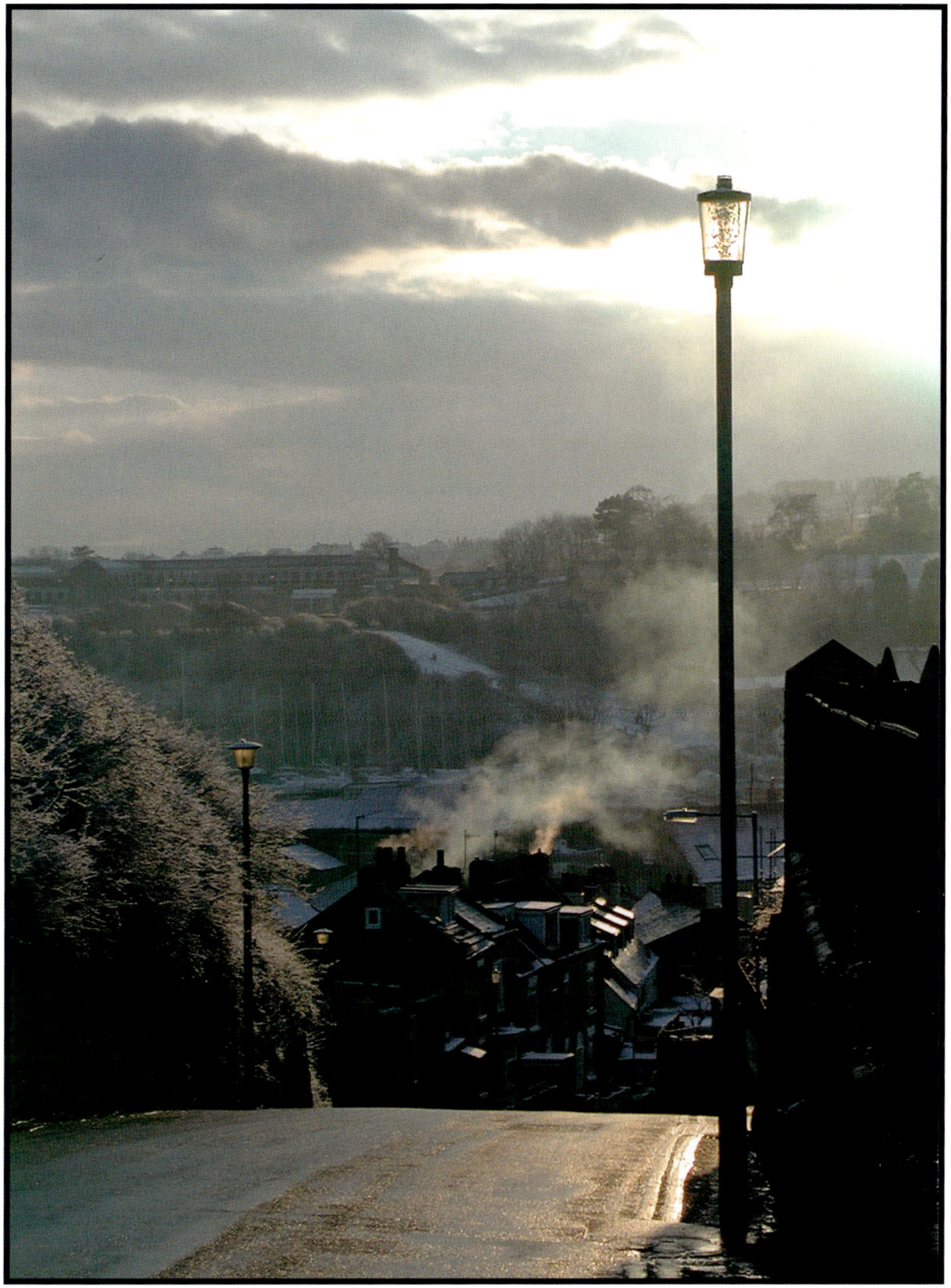

'Green Lane, Whitby'

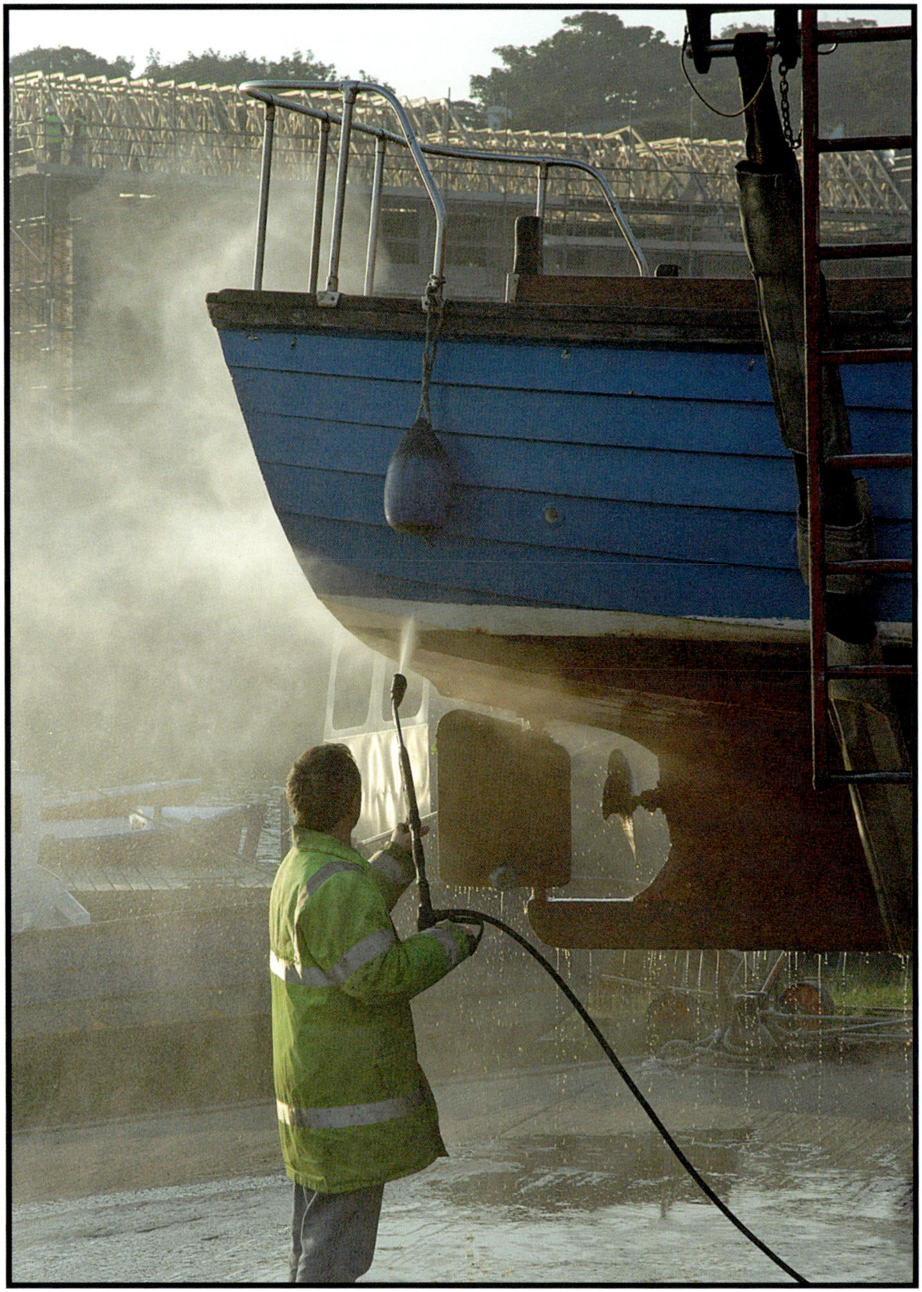

'Power wash'

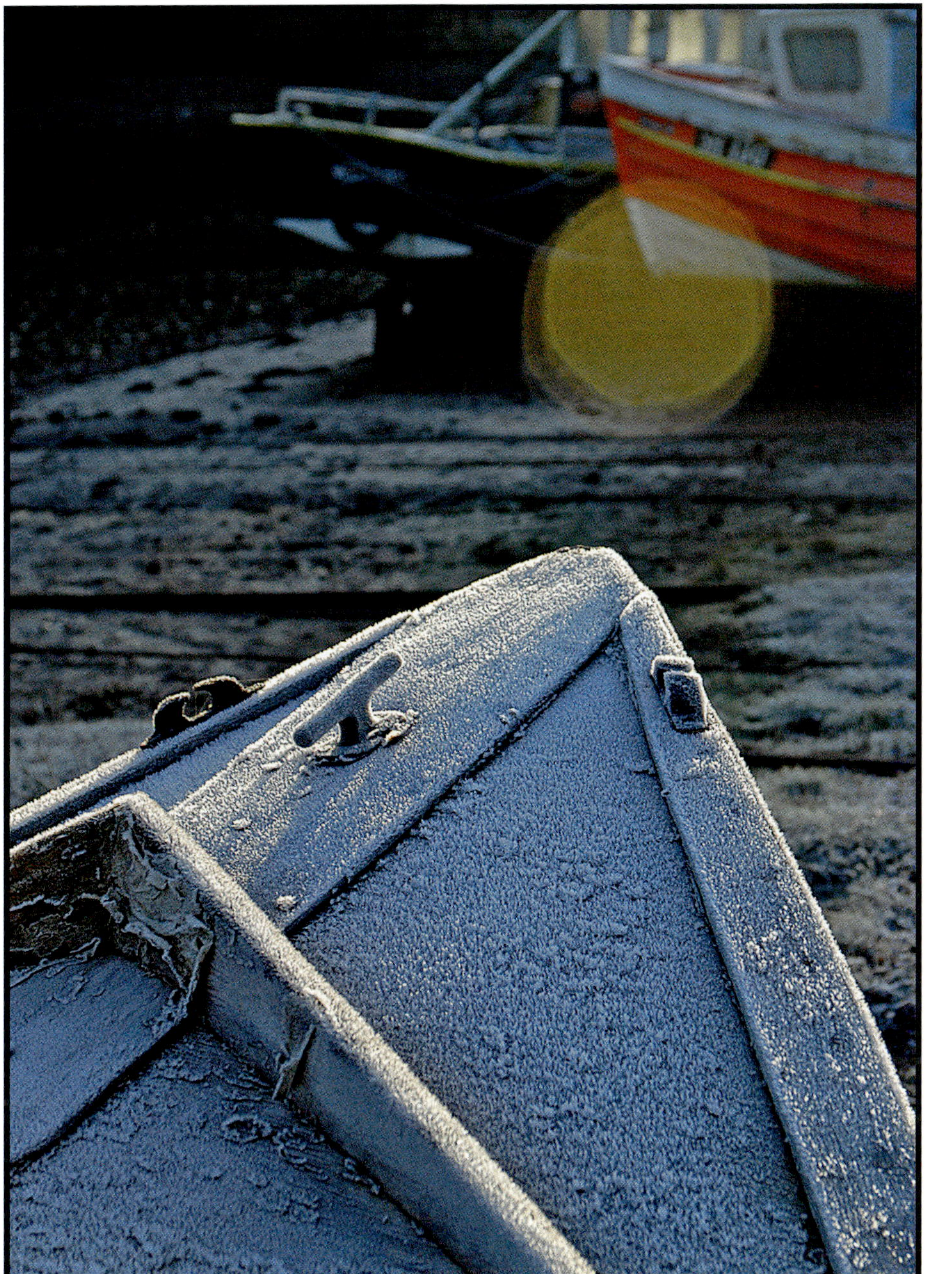

‘Cold front’

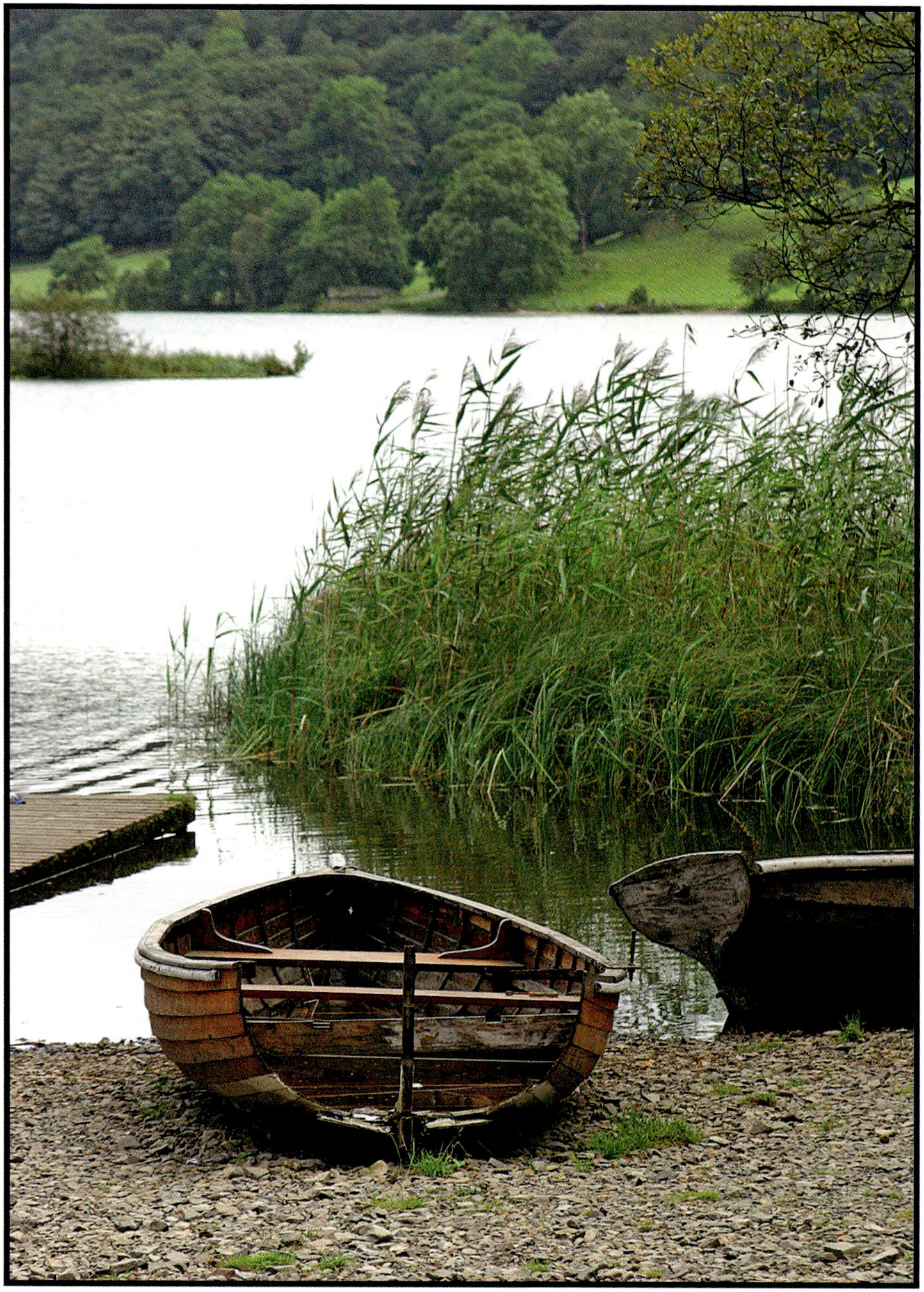

'Grasmere'

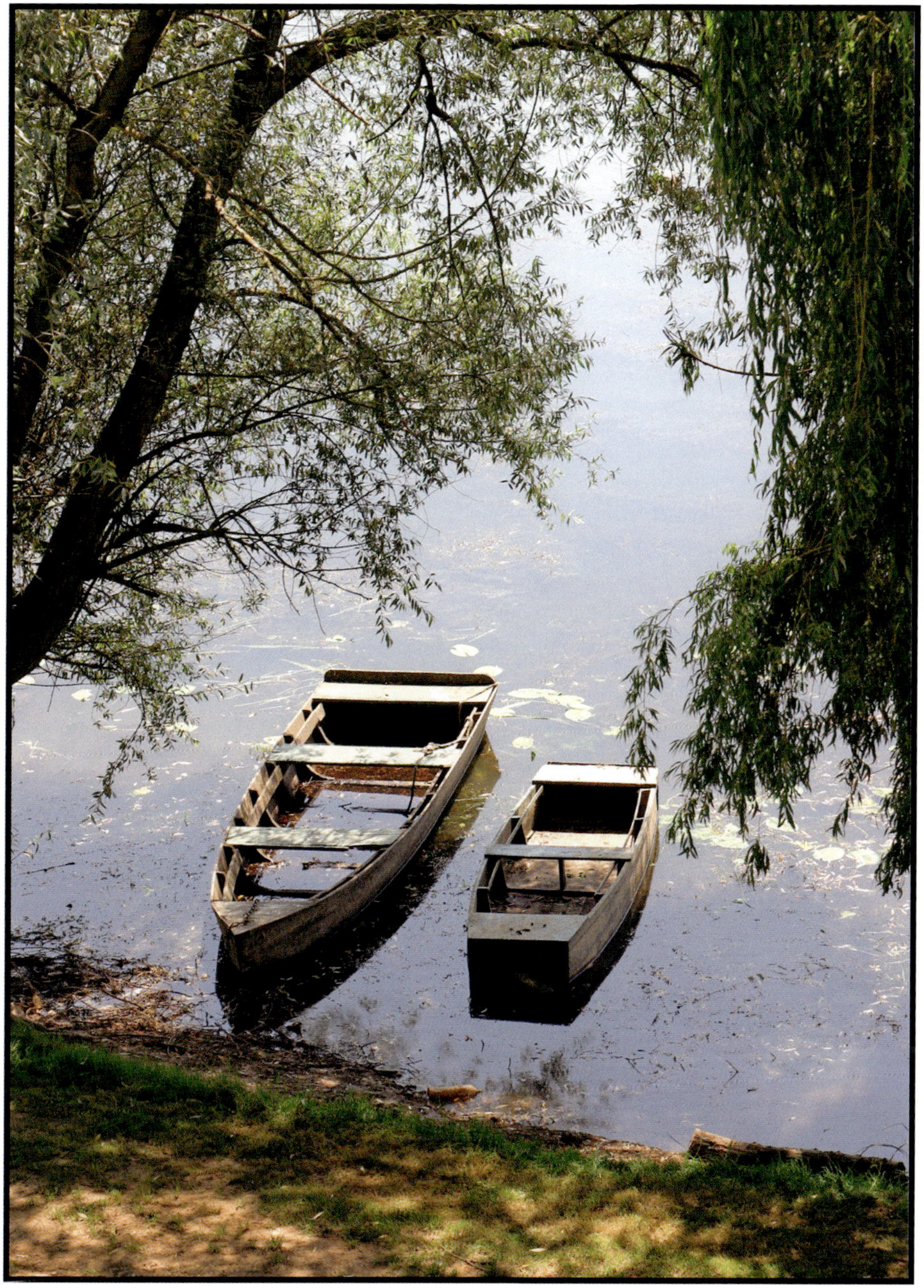

'Under the willow tree'

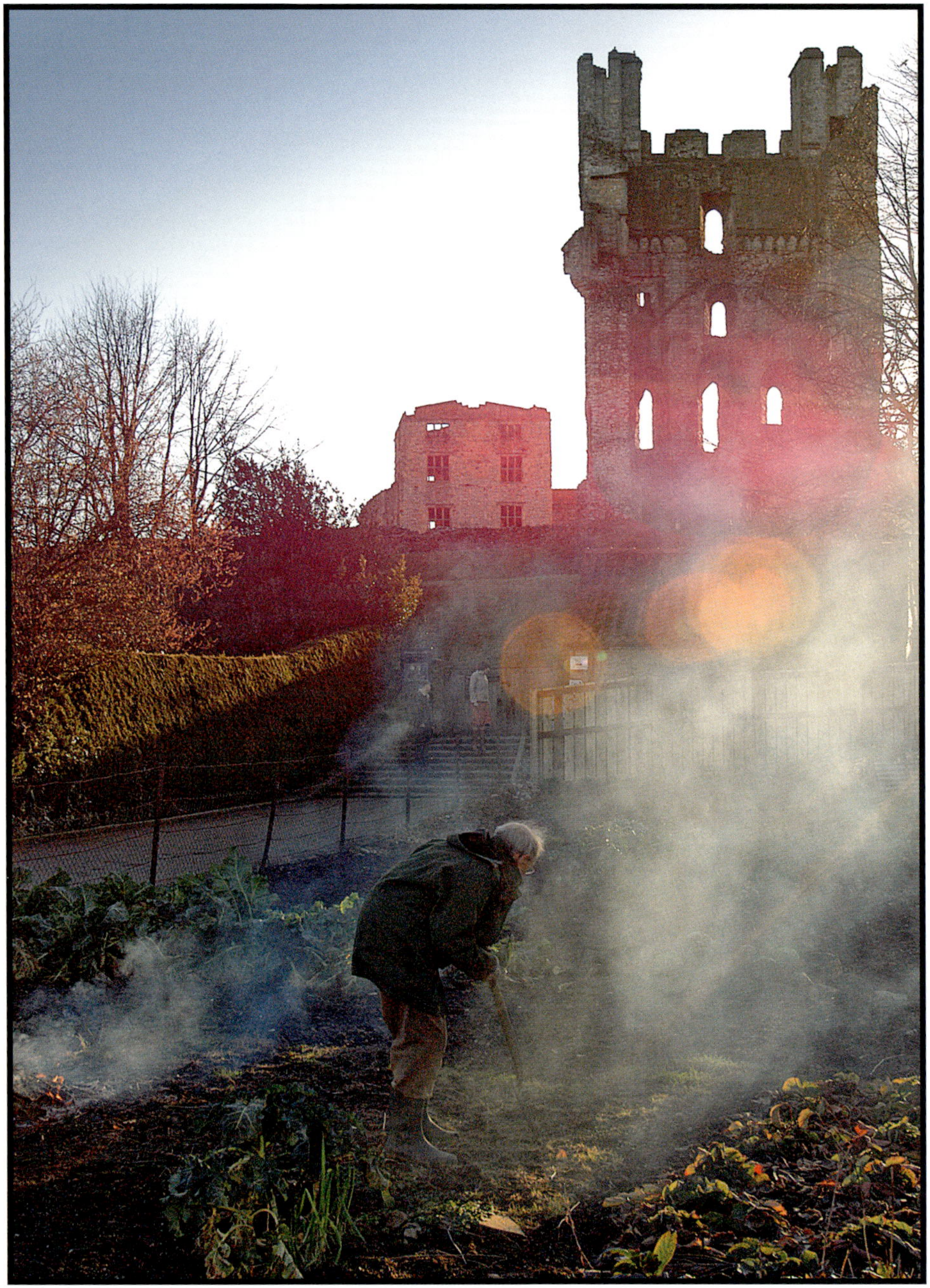

'Winter bonfire'

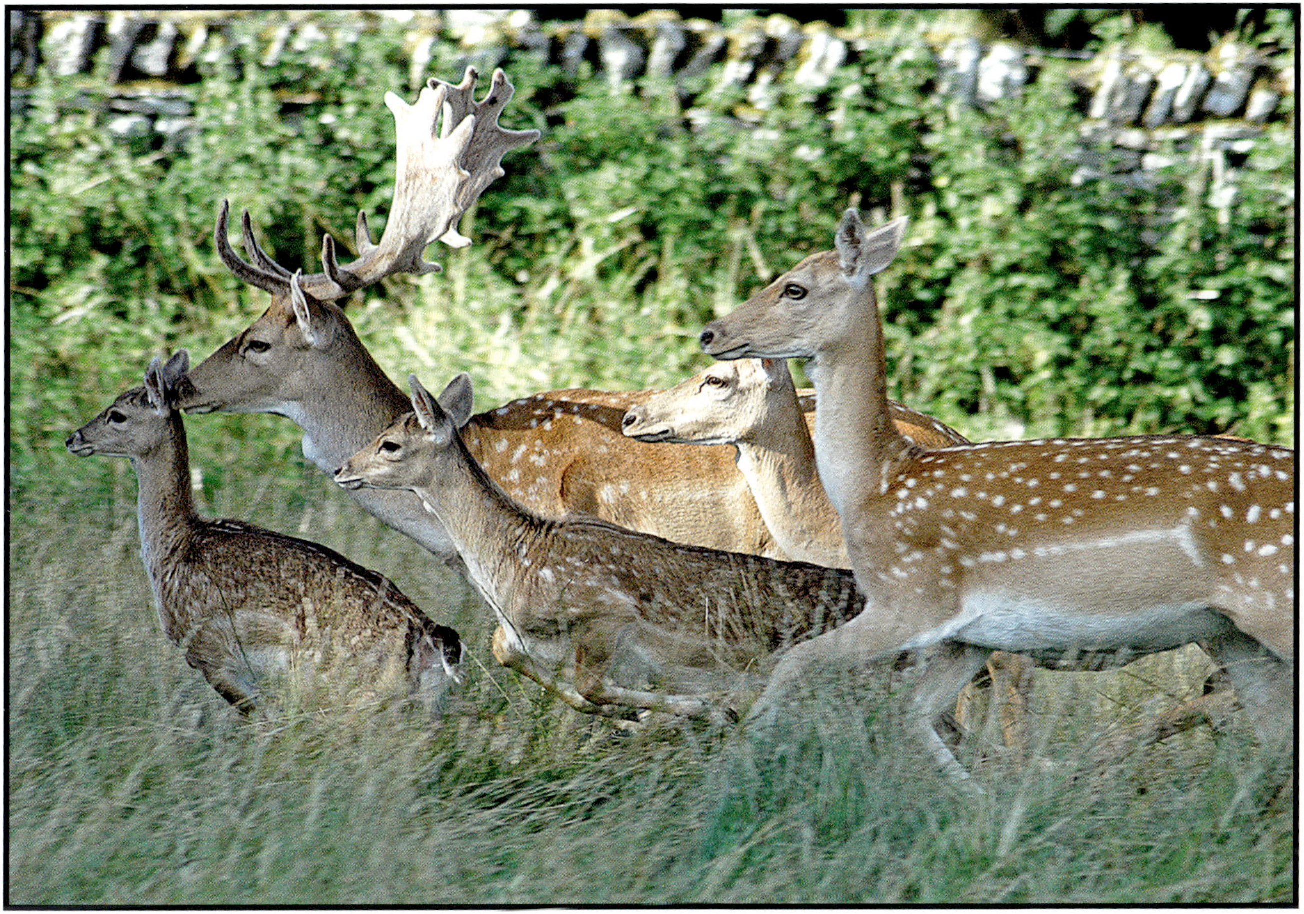

‘Running deer’

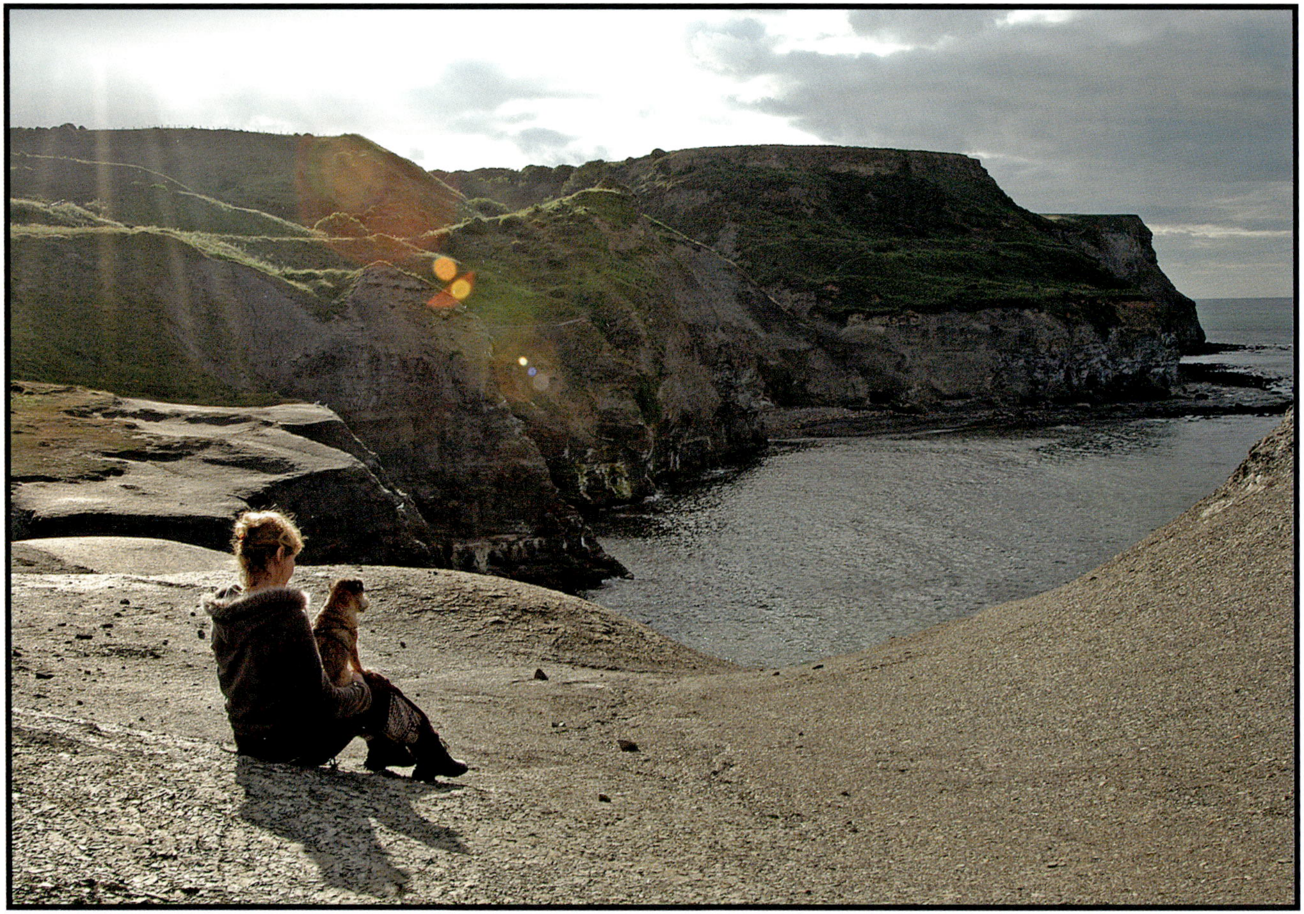

‘Sea of tranquility’

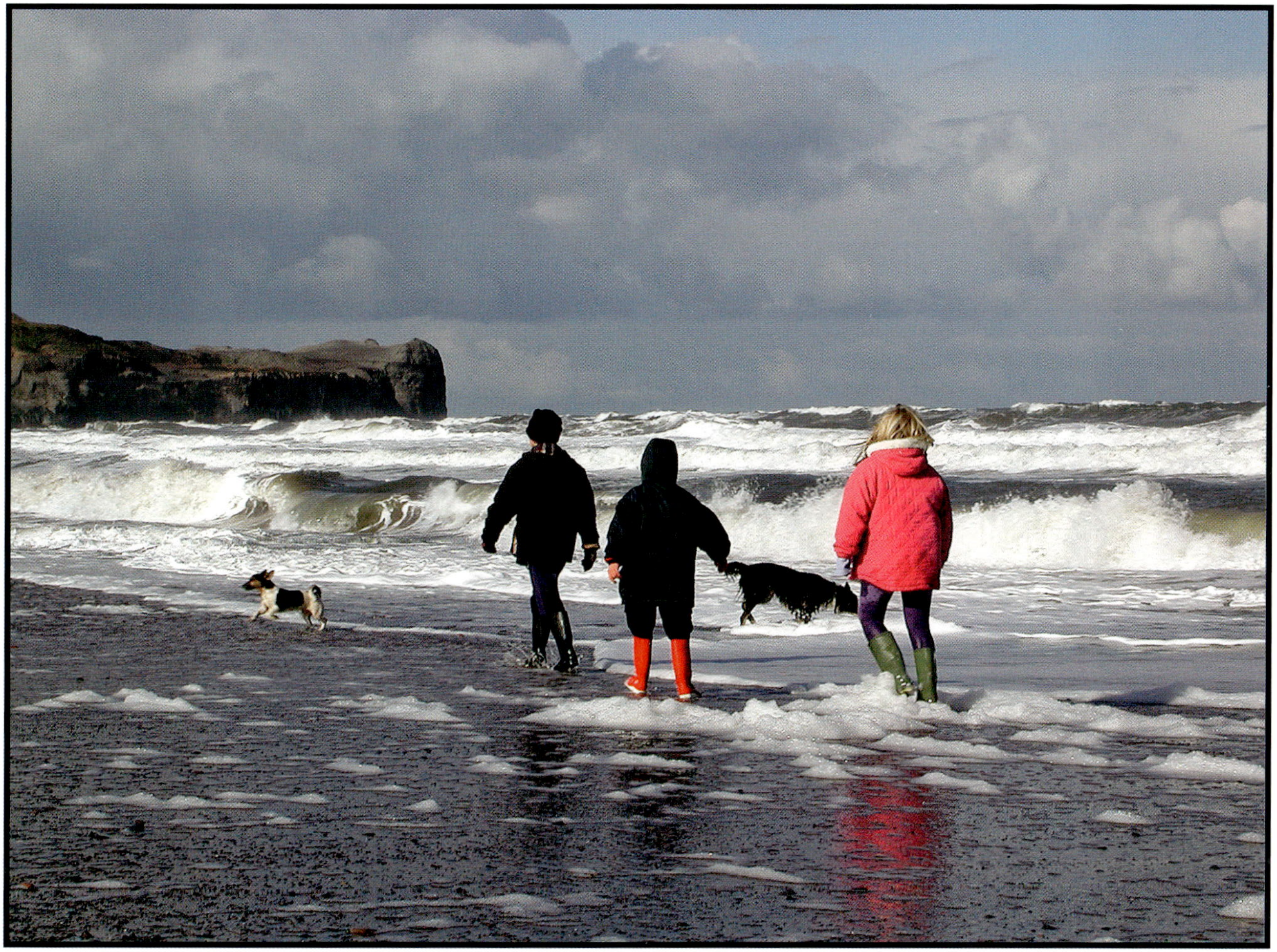

‘Bright new day’

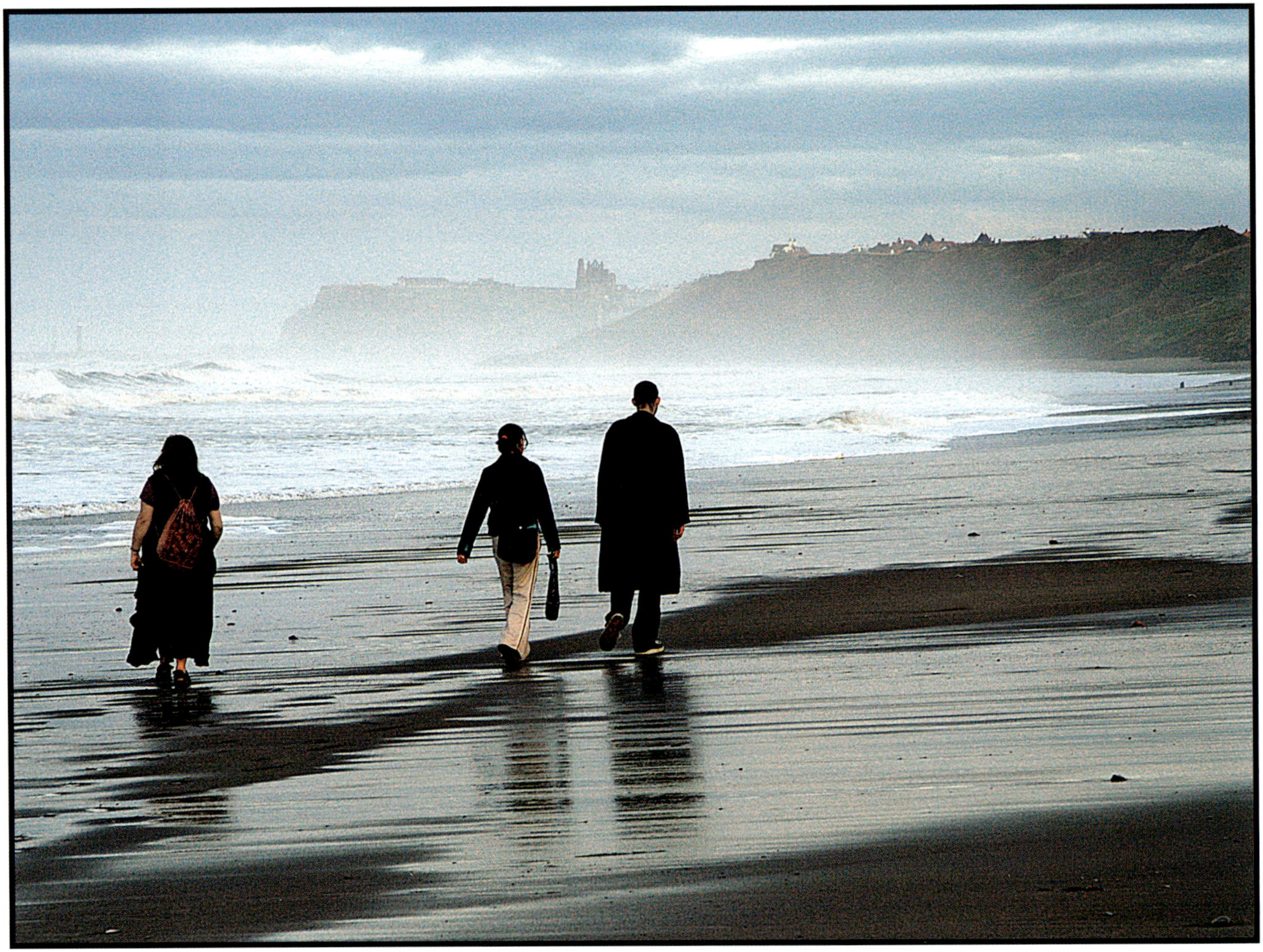

'Sea spray'

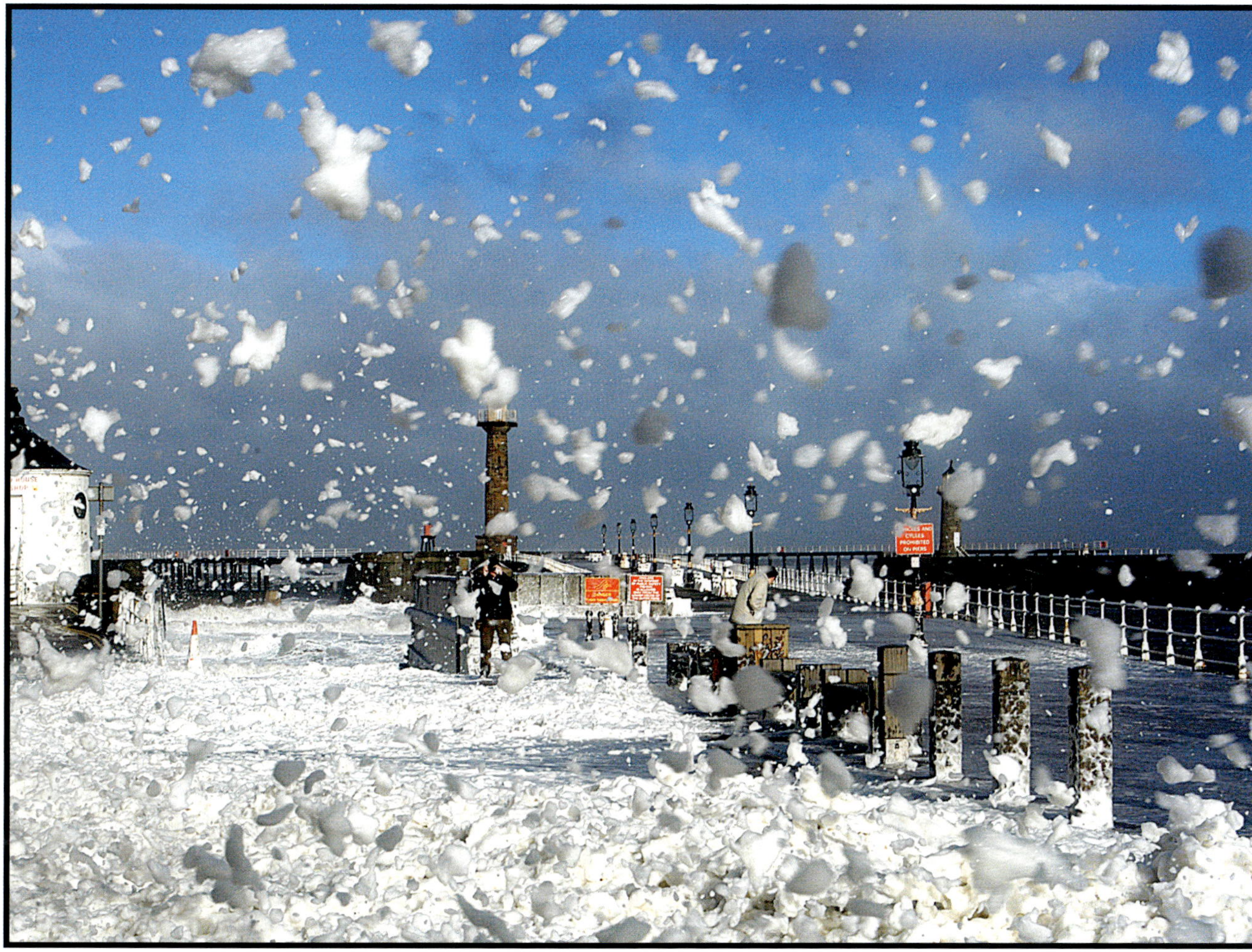

'Foaming at the harbour mouth'

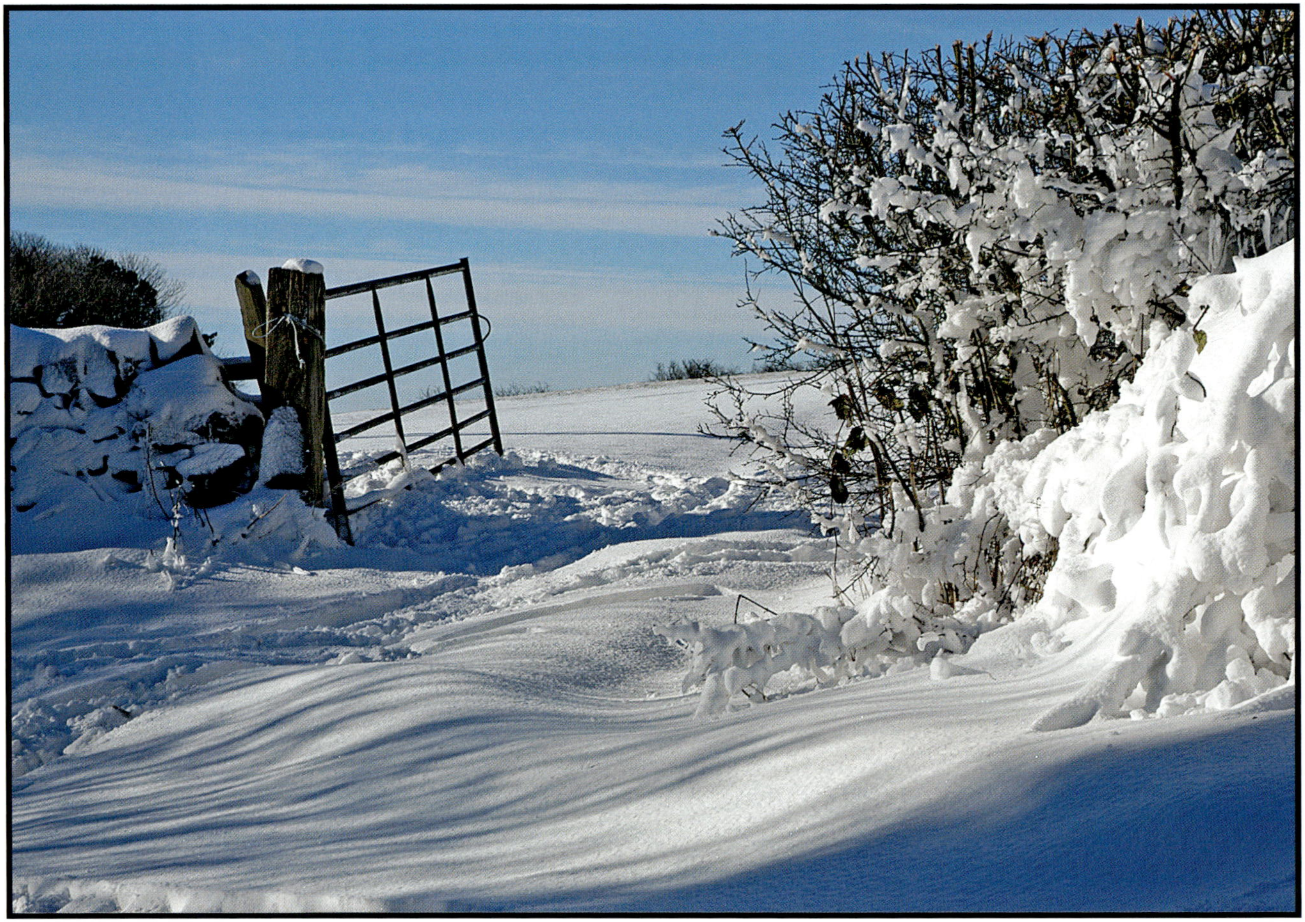

'Winter gateway'

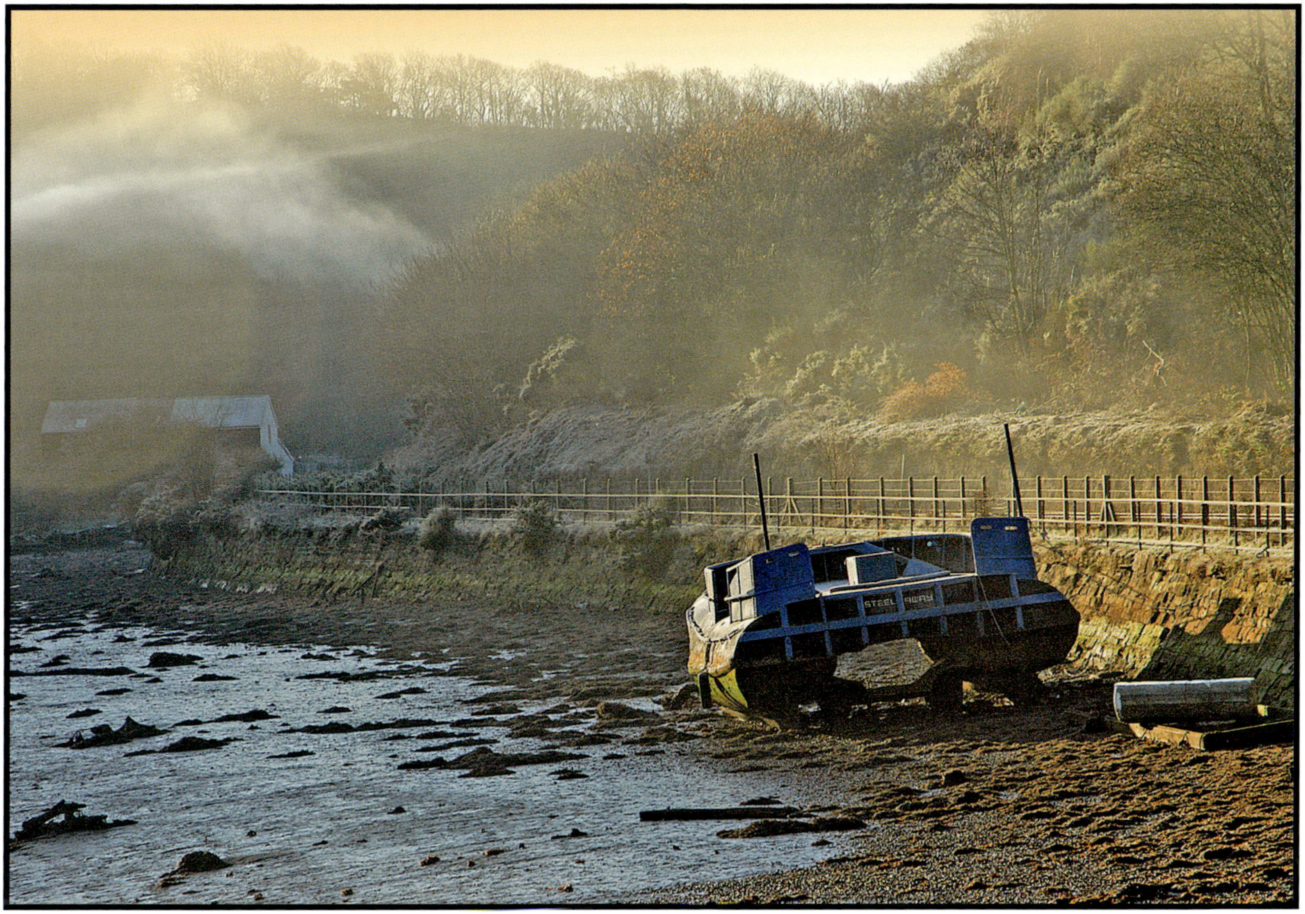

'Frosty morning, Whitby'

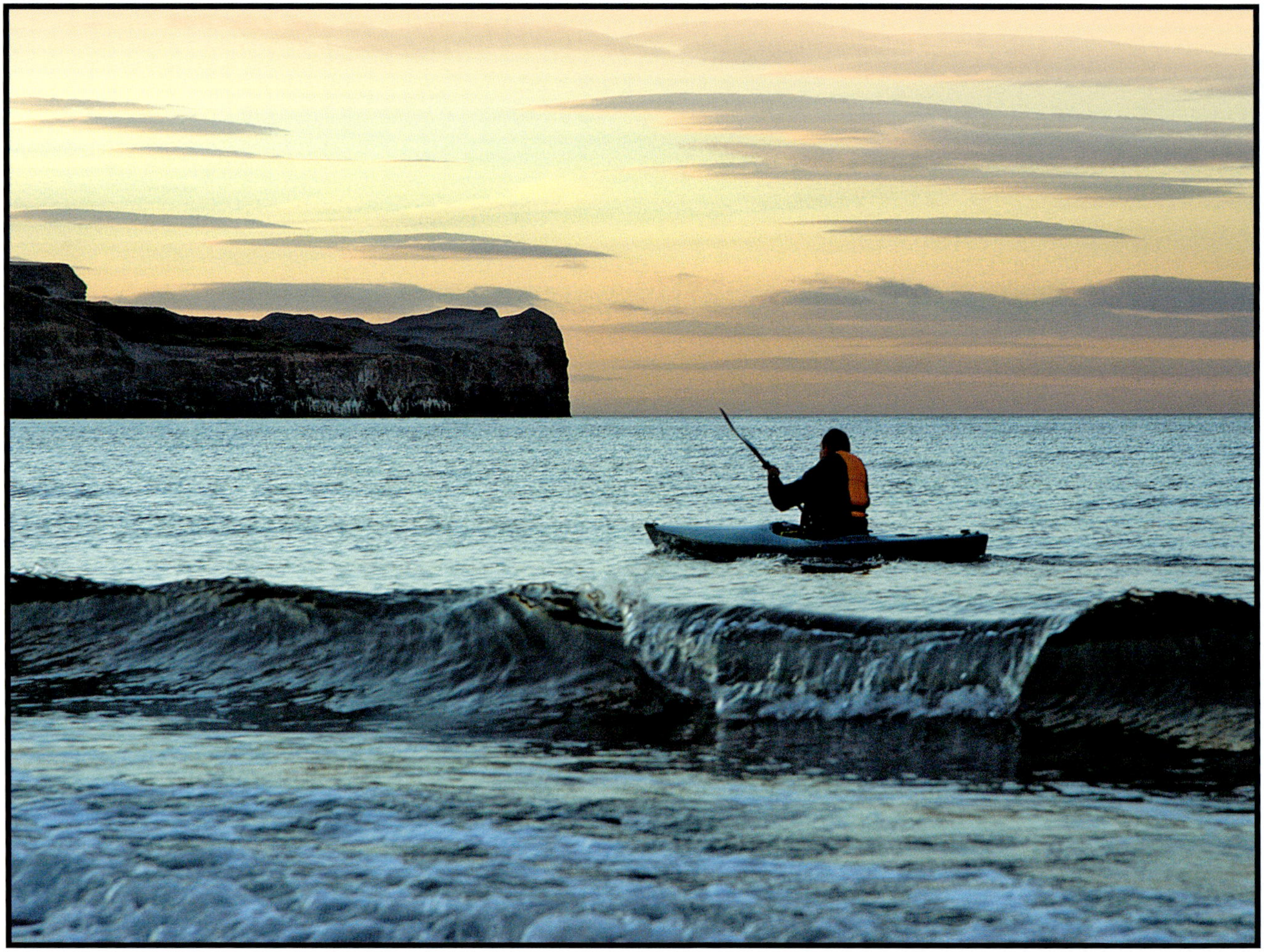

'On the crest of a wave'

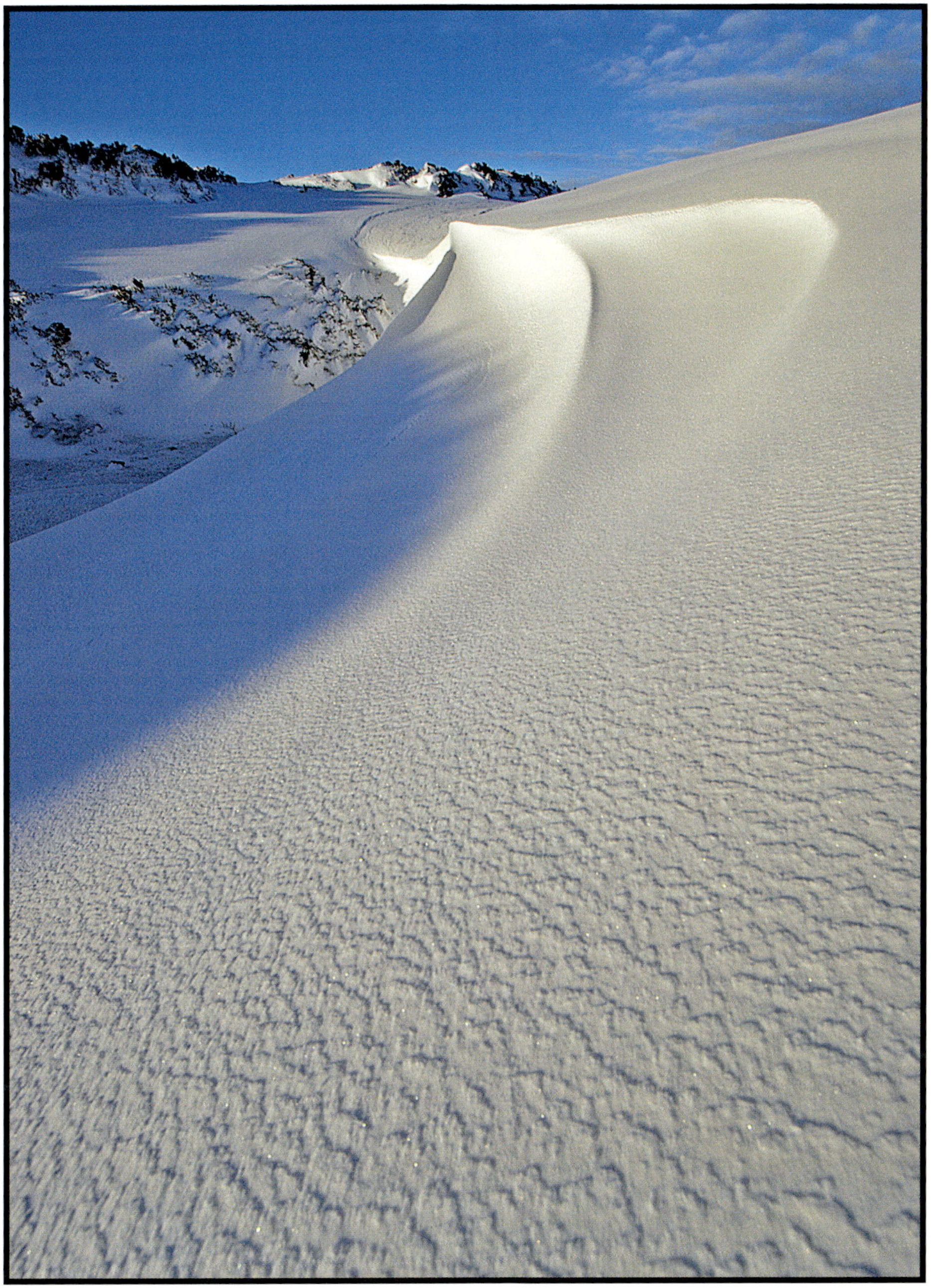

‘Big snow’

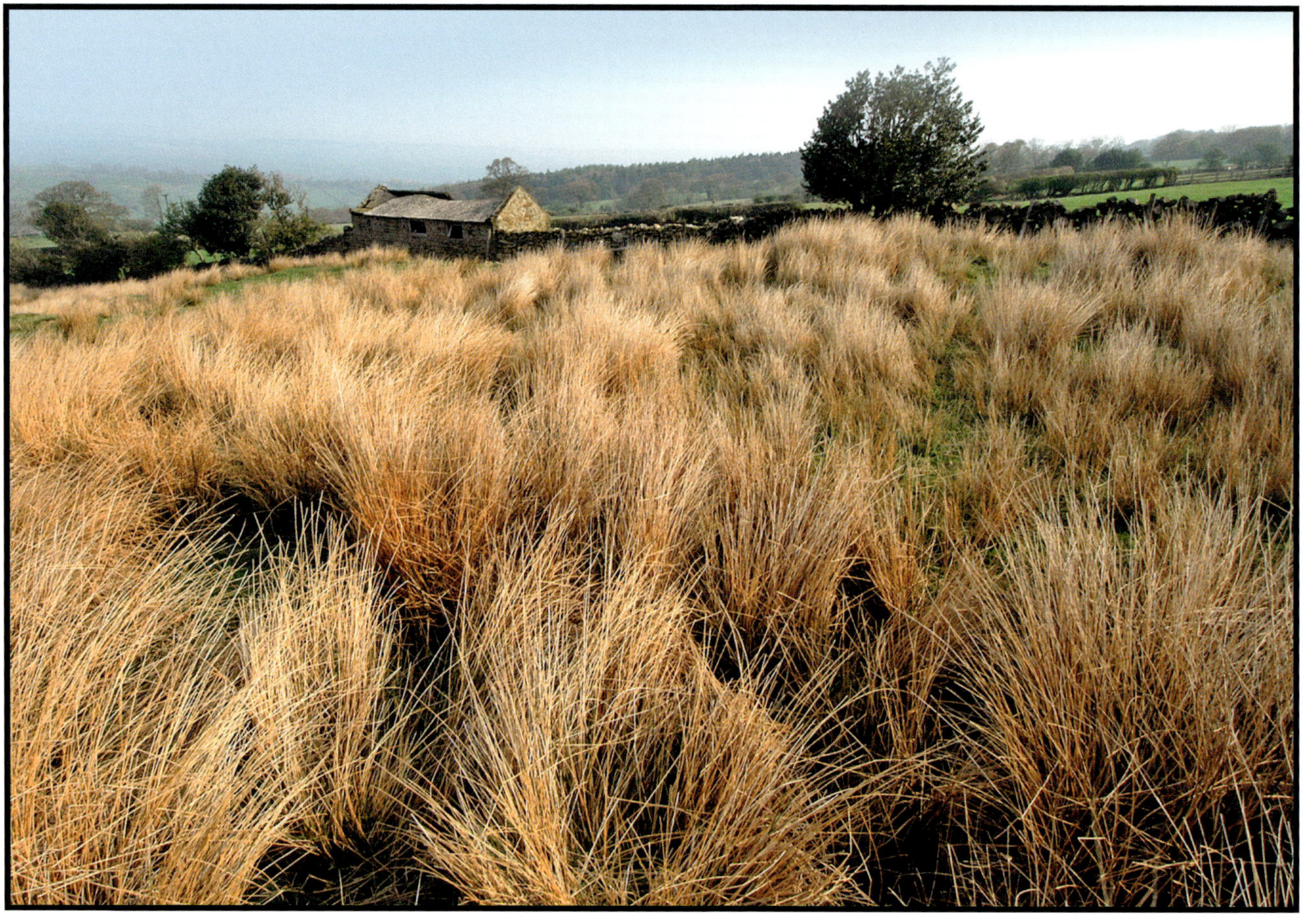

‘Green End, Goathland’

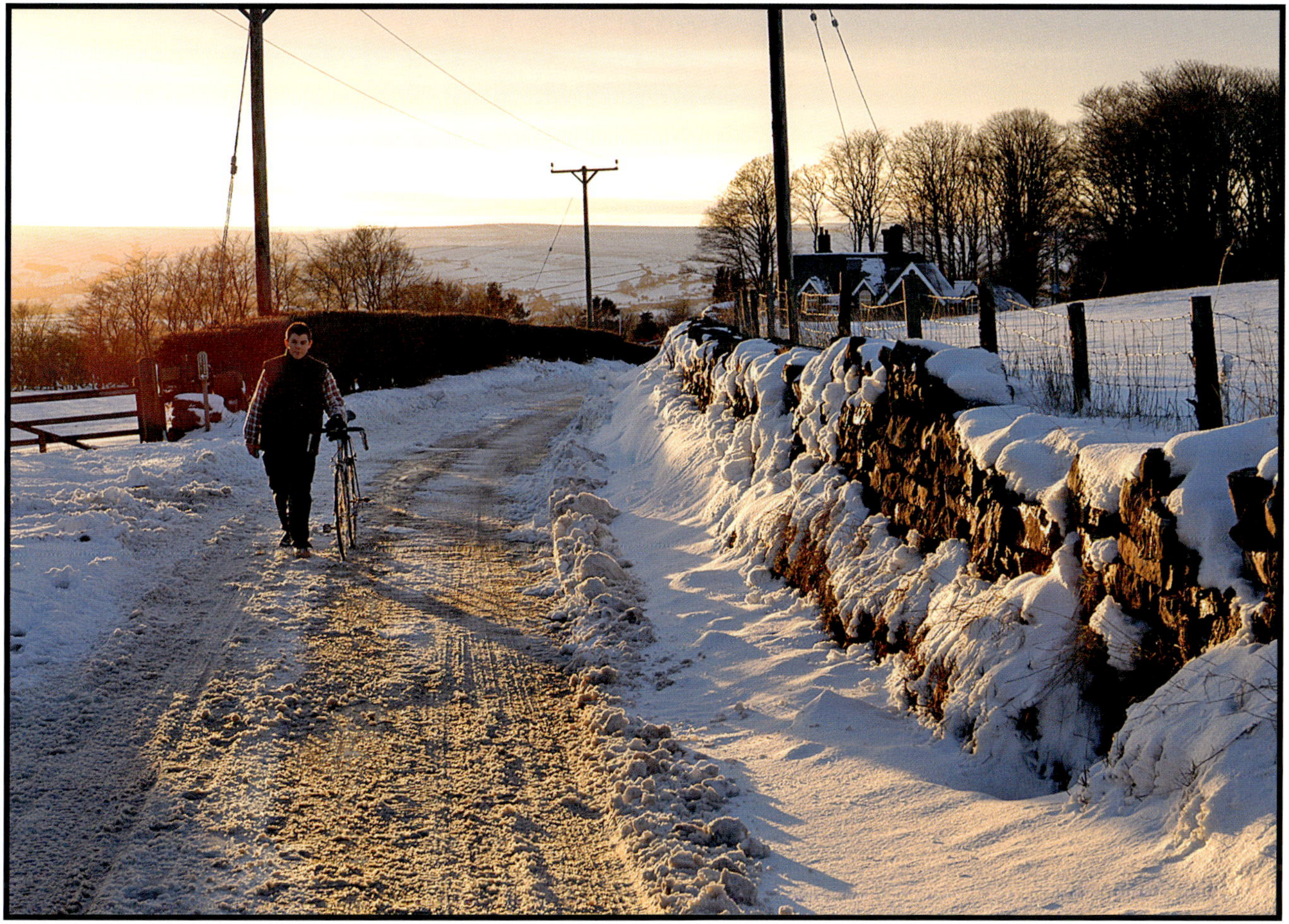

‘End of the day’